CIDER VINEGAR

Explains the many facets of cider vinegar, including its use in cooking and healing. With a selection of recipes and notes on the composition and manufacture of this 'miracle food'.

THORSONS NUTRIENTS FOR HEALTH

CIDER VINEGAR

—

The liquid with remarkable healing power

MAURICE HANSSEN

Thorsons
An Imprint of HarperCollins*Publishers*

Thorsons
An Imprint of HarperCollins*Publishers*
77–85 Fulham Palace Road,
Hammersmith, London W6 8JB

First published by Thorsons 1974
This edition 1995
3 5 7 9 10 8 6 4 2

© 1989 Thorsons Editiorial Board

A catalogue record for this book
is available from the British Library

ISBN 0 7225 3118 4

Printed and bound in Great Britain by
Caledonian International Book Manufacturing Ltd, Glasgow

CONTENTS

FOREWORD

When I first became acquainted with cider vinegar in the 1960s, I found it delicious. I also began to hear reports of its efficacy in the cure of a variety of minor health problems: it seemed to work well in the kinds of complaints that doctors call chronic, which means that they do not know how to cure them.

Despite numerous case histories of people who had found wonderful relief with cider vinegar in their day-to-day afflictions, the medical establishment often dismissed the claims of cider vinegar out of hand, as they were not part of a scientifically controlled trial.

It is now some fifteen years since I first became interested in cider vinegar, but its use for these conditions is as frequent as ever. It is also increasingly being used by farmers and horse breeders to treat animals.

Obviously, we need more scientific research to back up personal experience, but a wide variety of anecdotal sources would indicate that it works — from the folk medicine of New England to the work of Cyril Scott.

Whether your interest is in food that is both healthy and delicious, or in finding out if it works for you as a medicine, you cannot afford to be without *Cider Vinegar*.

Maurice Hanssen

Chapter 1

THE MAKING OF CIDER VINEGAR

In earlier times cider vinegar was frequently a welcome way of using cider that had gone sour. Today, such is the need for a reliable and effective product that there is no such easy way out for the producers. Three of the four main producers (Appleford, Martlet, Aspall and Whiteways) use a basically similar method with certain differences. The exception is Aspall who are employing a substantially different system for making cider vinegar from cider. All these firms have been most helpful in the preparation of this chapter and, indeed, in revealing helpful details from their private files regarding special uses and effects.

The apples arrive in September and October. Lorries full of freshly picked, specially grown, apples in the peak of condition. At Applefords the main crop is from the shiny Somerset cider apple, so full of minerals and acidity that it is not really possible to eat, even cooked with raw sugar! Martlet specialize in the firm fruity Bramley from the Kent and Sussex orchards, full of flavour and fragrance. Whiteways use Devon apples, not perhaps so tart as those from Somerset, but producing an excellent cider. Aspall have over eighty acres of organically maintained orchards in Suffolk from which they also make juice.

Until recently, after the whole apples had been coarsely chopped, they would be fed into hydraulic presses which sent volumes of delectable fresh apple juice coursing into cool, underground vats. The once-pressed pulp was then transferred to another press and squeezed until the apples became almost dry. Today, the apples go through an enormous rotary and continuous press which extracts the juice even more surely than the presses of old. When the apple remains reach the end, all the juice has gone and what is left is sent to be converted into organic compost or apple pectin. This is the setting agent used to provide the right consistency in good jams and conserves. It is good to know that the apple is so completely used for our health, nutrition and good eating.

The apple juice goes then into large vats, usually, of Russian oak because only those huge trees provide perfect staves of sufficient length and quality. A culture of yeast begins the fermentation which completely changes all the sugar in the apple juice into alcohol. The time this takes depends upon the temperature and on certain other factors, but is about 3-4 weeks. After this, cider needs to mature for about six months— much longer than the four or five weeks needed for beer in a brewery— and then we are ready to make the vinegar.

The final process is called acetification. The traditional process, which is now superseded, was to acetify in huge 20,000 gallon vats made of Columbian pine or New Zealand Kauri pine although there was no reason why the stainless steel or fibre glass vats or glass lined steel vats which are replacing them should not be just as good. The vat had a web of lathes upon which sterilized four-feet layers of birch twigs were put until the vat contained some two tons of twigs. These were steamed for forty-eight hours prior to use. The twigs were then soaked in alcohol from cider mixed with some vinegar that was from a freshly working vat. This allowed the micro-organism, a bacterium called *Acetobacter* to become well established on the birch twigs.

The cider was then added in 5,000 gallon batches and circulated through the acetifier for two or three weeks. This allowed plenty of oxygen to be present which is necessary for the *Acetobacter* to convert entirely the alcohol into acetic acid. When this process had been completed the vinegar was lightly filtered into storage vats, of aged oak , where it developed flavour and any sediment was thrown.

Today, the invention of the 'Fring's Acetator' has speeded up the changing of alcohol into acetic acid without any loss of quality. In fact, there is every chance that quality is increased in modern cider vinegars because the enclosed Fring's process very much reduces the loss of the vital ingredients by evaporation, which often occurred in the traditional method.

In the Fring's Acetator the Acetobacter grows in a suspension of fine air bubbles and fermenting liquid. This causes a very even distribution of the Acetobacter through the cider and the change, under carefully controlled conditions, takes only a few days. Half the tank is usually ready to use whilst the other half is being transformed, so the result is a more or less continuous supply of high quality cider vinegar. Both processes produce an acetic acid content which depends on the efficiency of the equipment but is usually around 7 per cent. This is far too strong for normal use so it is then diluted to about 4.8 per cent before being bottled. (See analyses for further information.)

The production at Martlet has increased so much over the past years that they have now installed a very advanced Fring's Acetator called the 'Continuo'. As the name implies, this produces a continual supply of cider vinegar and it is much more efficient to use than the old batch process. The 'Continuo' is especially suitable for lower strengths of vinegar, and is thus especially valuable in preserving the high mineral content that we look for in our best products.

Aspall use the 'Greenshields' process for the continuous production of their vinegar, and Rod Greenshields of the University of Aston, a distinguished expert in fermentation technology, with his engineer brother Michael, told me about their machines with great enthusiasm.

The 'Greenshields' process was developed at the University of Aston in Birmingham by Francis Harmon Limited and is covered by a British patent. The apparatus is made of high-grade plastic and uses a tubular fermenter through which passes a stream of bubbles. There are no moving parts and the fermenting liquid passes through it continuously, allowing the Acetobacter to grow and produce the vinegar naturally and without forced agitation.

Aspall were the first company to introduce this plant for the production of cider vinegar which, like Fring's system, has high efficiency, reduces losses and also minimizes the loss of vital constituents of the cider vinegar. The 'Greenshields' system has great flexibility because the Acetobacter can still be maintained in healthy condition even when the air is stopped. This process is ideally suitable for both the smallest cider vinegar producer and the larger manufacturer.

Once in a bottle, it is important that the vinegar does not oxydize or grow moulds. For this reason it was usual to add a substance which deters the oxygen from affecting the vinegar. This is sulphur dioxide, E220. This was first known to have been used some 2,000 years ago by the ancient Greeks who burnt sulphur in the top of barrels of wine before sealing them down. The U.K. Foods Laws state that the maximum allowable content of sulphur dioxide in cider vinegar is 200 parts per million, which is much too high a level in our opinion as malt vinegar is permitted only 70 parts per million. We would not recommend the use of cider vinegar containing sulphite preservatives.

As knowledge of good production practice has increased, fortunately most manufacturers have been able to avoid the use of sulphites which can cause asthma attacks, although it is quite safe in moderate amounts for most of us. Sometimes a little vitamin C (ascorbic acid) is used and it is to the credit of these manufacturers that they use such healthy methods for maintaining the quality of their products.

Martlet cider vinegar is sold in its natural, light straw-coloured state, as is that of Aspall and Whiteways. Appleford make both a golden and a darker variety which is coloured with a little burnt sugar caramel to a pleasing rich brown.

The change of the alcohol into vinegar (acetic acid) follows this chemical chain:

$$CH_3CH_2OH \xrightarrow{-2H} CH_3CHO \xrightarrow{(0)} CH_3COOH$$

$$\text{ethyl alcohol} \qquad \text{acetaldehyde} \qquad \text{acetic acid}$$

The greatest possible yield of 1.3 grams of acetic acid from 1.0 gram of alcohol is nearly reached in modern equipment.

Chapter 2

CHOOSING THE RIGHT CIDER VINEGAR

As you will have read in the first chapter, cider vinegar is just vinegar made from cider. The shopper has many makes to choose from. Which is best?

In Britain there are four main producers, Appleford, Martlet, Whiteways and Aspall. These are all makers of different cider vinegars of the very highest quality. The main producers all also do some bottling for other firms. If cider vinegar is imported the country of origin is stated on the label and some good French products are available. The tests and results of this book were all made using British cider vinegars. Dr Jarvis has obtained good results with his American products.

Whiteways and Aspall call their vinegar 'cyder', whilst Martlet and Appleford call theirs 'cider'. Although Whiteways are probably Britain's oldest producer, they have been making it for more than 100 years, the 'cyder' spelling is not significant. In fact from the earliest times writers have been in two minds (or more) over the spelling. Neither is incorrect, as you will find if you examine the history of the name. There was a late Latin word *sicera*, which meant intoxicating liquor or strong drink.

This was often used in the Bible of that time. In due course the word became altered, first to *sizra* and then to *sidra*.

Apples are a native fruit of Britain, in fact it is thought to be one of the only fruits to spread from East to West.

Some of the old names for varieties of cider apples charmingly remind us of an earlier era. Favourites include *Avalon, Sweet Alford, Kingston Black, White Close Pippin, Yarlington Mill, Ponsford, Fair Maid of Devon, Cap of Liberty, Porter's Perfection* and, perhaps cheekily or perhaps because even in those days cider was thought of as helping people to slim — *Slack Ma Girdle*!

There may well have been cultivated orchards in Britain since Neolithic times for cider making. In the thirteenth-century the bailiff's account of the Earl of Devon's estate at Exminster showed a large production of cider. In 1724, Daniel Defoe, of *Robinson Crusoe* fame, wrote that 'Between Topsham and Axminster so much fruit grew and so much cider was made that sometimes they send to London between ten and twenty thousand hogshead of cider each year'. A hogshead is approximately 60 gallons (275 litres). No doubt cider making began on a large scale as a way of preserving the goodness of apples and, indeed, vitamin C, through the winter months.

Literature began to refer commonly to cider in the fourteenth-century. Interesting references include the following:

1398— Trevisa wrote, 'Honey cometh of floures, sidre of frute and ale of corne'.

1497— Bishop Alcock wrote, 'Saynt John Baptyst wich ete neuer flesshe, dranke no wyne nor cydre'.

1626— Francis Bacon wrote about sider; in 1663 Boyle talked of syder and perry.

1708— J. Phillips wrote, 'My mill now grinds choice apples and the British vats o'erflow with generous cider'.

1767— Hutchinson wrote, 'A barrel full of cyder'. In his *History of England* at about the same time, Macaulay recorded, 'Hogsheads of their best cyder'.

1875— Jevons wrote, 'The farm labourer may partially receive payment in cider'.

So the different spellings change from age to age and run simultaneously together without there being a particular regional or other significance. You can therefore use, with a clear conscience, cyder or cider vinegar!

The cost has, considering the general way in which money has been devalued over the last 75 years, remained remarkably modest. In 1906, Whiteways listed apple vinegar in champagne bottles at a trade price of 7/6d (37½ pence) a dozen. Similar sizes, which are by far the most economical if you use a lot, are perhaps 30 times as much today. When you remember that a goodish working wage was £50 a year in 1907, cider vinegar is not at all expensive today.

THE BASIC TREATMENT

The standard way in which to take cider vinegar is to mix two teaspoonsful in a tumbler of cold or warm water. Take one glassful first thing in the morning, one during or after lunch and one in the evening.

Different users find that different makes of cider vinegar work best for them so, if the first one you try does not seem to produce the hoped-for results, then try another. Some people with sensitive stomachs may find two teaspoonsful too much for them. In such cases, start with one teaspoonful until you are used to the effects.

Children under the age of about eight years also usually find the small dose sufficient. Infants can, of course, use less still but many babies and children really enjoy vinegar! A sweet tooth tends to be developed by the parents because they associate sweetness with reward. This is not to the advantage of a child's health — a 'vinegar tooth' is far better with a preference for savoury foods.

HONEY AND CIDER VINEGAR

For many, a mixture of honey and cider vinegar is ideal. Best seems to be equal volumes of the two ingredients. By weight this is equivalent to 42 per cent of cider vinegar and 58 per cent of honey.

This is very much an individual thing. Many who find cider vinegar either upsetting their stomach or not working well, find the mixture, which can be obtained in a prepared form, the perfect answer. If you mix your own, be sure to use an unblended pure honey. It does not matter if it is set or clear. Do *not* heat the mixture, as this is not good for certain constituents. The mixture is especially useful for relieving the symptoms of hay fever and for asthma. The honey is soothing and helps lubricate the throat.

Chapter 3

THE COMPOSITION OF CIDER VINEGAR

The active principles in cider vinegar come from the combination of minerals, organic matter and acetic acid in a naturally produced blend. There are certain to be fluctuations from time to time because of variations in the apple. Different vinegars suit different persons depending upon the balance required.

The figures quoted are in grammes (g) per 100 millilitres (ml) or, where appropriate, in milligrammes (mg) or parts per million (p.p.m.)

Appleford—analysis per 100 ml

Total solid matter	3.31g
Acetic acid	4.75g
Sugars (as invert)	0.45g
Mineral ash	0.32g
Tannins	0.015g
Calcium	8.2mg
Phosphorus	4.85mg
Sodium	7.0mg

Potassium	100mg
Riboflavin (vitamin B2)	trace
Nicotinic Acid	trace
Iron	0.05p.p.m.
Copper	0.025p.p.m.

Martlet—analysis per 100ml

Total solid matter	1.36g
Acetic Acid	5.40g
Sugars (as invert)	0.40g
Mineral ash	0.24g
Tannins	0.002g
Protein	0.08g
Calcium	7.1mg
Phosphorus	6.5mg
Sodium	12.0mg
Potassium	103.0mg
Iron	1.3mg
Copper	0.54 p.p.m.
Zinc	0.10 p.p.m.
Riboflavin (vitamin B2)	trace
Nicotinic Acid	0.02mg

Whiteways—analysis per 100ml

Total solid matter	2.70g
Acetic Acid	5.51g
Sugars (as invert)	0.50g
Sugar Free Dry Extract	2.19g
Mineral Ash	0.22g
Tannins	0.42g
Protein	0.06g
Calcium	4.8mg
Phosphorus	4.7mg
Sodium	3.24mg
Potassium	85.3mg
Iron	0.2mg
Copper	0.01mg
Zinc	0.05mg
Riboflavin (vitamin B2)	trace

Nicotinic Acid	trace
Ascorbic Acid (vitamin C)	150 p.p.m.

Some Continental cider vinegars are made by using a very strong alcohol cider as the starting material, making the resulting acid content as high as thirteen or fourteen per cent, and then diluting the whole lot with water down to the normal acidity levels. This does, of course, mean that the mineral contents are reduced.

The analyses of these three main makes of vinegar are entirely satisfactory for our purposes. It all depends which suits you as to which you use.

Aspall cider vinegar is another excellent product of good analytical quality as well as being organically grown.

Chapter 4

CIDER VINEGAR FOR HEALTH

Describing the remarkable reports praising cider a friend said in a scathing tone, 'Cider Vinegar seems to cure everything except corns!' It is true that it has many uses. But, to draw a lesson from this rebuke we would say to you that corns do not usually trouble people with perfect shoes. In the same way, illness is minimized in a perfectly fit body.

Fitness comes from having sufficient exercise, enough sleep, a realistic and positive attitude of mind and a *well managed diet*. Cider vinegar contains minute quantities of minerals which help some to adjust their metabolism or bodily processes that are frequently missing when we eat.

That grand old pioneer of German natural medicine in the last century, Father Sebastian Kneipp, had the right attitude when he said that, if a person came to him with an open ulcer in the leg he would begin the treatment by looking at what his patient ate, then correct his diet because the ulcer is only the outward sign of an inward inbalance which must be corrected to achieve a real cure. We are often all too ready to rush to the medicine chest when we should be looking at our lifestyle as well. Cider vinegar has been called a panacea. Not because it has a strong drug-like action with unwelcome and often unsuspected side effects, but because cider vinegar makes the body normal.

Also for this reason cider vinegar cannot be guaranteed to work every time for everybody. But it *does* work, and work marvellously, for hundreds and thousands of men, women and children throughout the world.

Dr Jarvis carried out some experiments on cows to see if, as had been thought, it was the phosphorus in cider vinegar which was the vital and required element. It was not, and the final answer must await trials which will cost a great deal of money to carry out and which will not alter the fact which you can profit by straight away — that it really works for a very large number of people.

The data that formed the basis of this book was drawn from over a thousand unsolicited letters written by satisfied users of cider vinegar. It was in no sense a scientific trial, but the positive way in which millions of consumers, using cider vinegar for both humans and animals, continue to arrive at the same conclusions will encourage others to try cider vinegar for themselves. This work was done with Appleford's Cider Apple Vinegar. Martlet have carried out successful controlled trials using a mixture of honey and cider vinegar for the treatment of hay fever and of asthma. Martlet, Whiteways, Appleford and Aspall have each much experience in the veterinary uses. It is this last usage, for animals, that convinces us that the use of cider vinegar is not strange or unreasonable. We simply do not believe that animals can be fooled into health through cider vinegar. They recover because it works and, if it works for them, why should it not for us?

We shall discuss the results of the survey and the recommended dosages under each category of complaint but, for the sake of interest, here are the various uses and the numbers of users in each main section:

General Health (Vigour, happiness, etc.)	426
General Qualities and Benefits	214
Slimming	184
Cooking	38
Rheumatism	39
Arthritis	39
'Flu, Colds, Catarrh, Sore Throat	16
Wrinkles	2

Blood Purification	2
Hay Fever	14
Toe and Finger Nails	4
Backache	4
Varicose Veins	4
Asthma	11
Skin Troubles	2
Insomnia	7
Digestive Disturbances	34
Cataract	1
Heart Troubles	17
Cramp	4
Shingles	5
High Blood Pressure	12
	1,079

Remember, as you read the descriptions of the various complaints, that they are *all* based on actual case histories supported by the experience of previous writers and users over very many years. Also, we will take this opportunity of thanking Appleford, Martlet, Whiteways and Aspall for the help they have given in the compilation of this comprehensive book on cider vinegar therapy. But we must also thank them and others for making this remarkable food available. Other countries also have cider vinegars of great quality. If you are not in Britain, experiment to find a type to suit you and your body's needs.

SLIMMING

Life assurance companies have known for a long time from their carefully kept records that fatness and health do not often go together.

Fatness does not look very attractive, at least not to Western eyes, and more children are unable to adjust to a happy school relationship with their fellows because they are ungraceful and ungainly fatties.

Cider vinegar can help you to achieve a normal diet. It improves the functioning and adjustment of the body so that there is efficient use made of the food you eat and you become very satisfied and content with the right amount.

Before embarking on your slimming with cider vinegar be sure to examine your present diet to see that it is well balanced and healthy. Cider vinegar can do a lot for you, but it is better if your provide yourself with the right nutritious diet as well. Check yourself:

1. Do I eat wholemeal bread and flour products? There is now over-whelming evidence that some of the diseases of western civiliza-tion, especially those in the colon or lower part of the gut, are caused by not taking enough cereal fibre. Apart from the nutrients present in foods it is now certain that its physical quality is also important to health. So the day when we can live on a diet of space-age pills may never arrive. Thank goodness for that!

2. Do I eat too much sugar? (The average intake of sugar in the U.K. is about 100 pounds (45 kilos) a year. That is for every man, woman and child. Some don't have their share, so many must have far more. Sugar, apart from making you fat, helps cause tooth decay, affects the blood and may cause heart trouble in some people.)

3. Am I sure to eat some green vegetable and some fruit each day? (Fruit, especially citrus, provides vitamin C. Vegetables are best lightly cooked or steamed in the minimum of water. Use the stock for soups as it contains water soluble vitamins and minerals.)

4. Do I include protein in my daily diet? (Protein builds muscles and repairs the cells. It cannot be stored for long so is needed daily. Proteins come from nuts, soya beans, milk, eggs, cheese, fish and lean meat.)

5. Do I eat too much salt? (If the circulation is sluggish, salt tends to increase the retention of water in the body. Try using smaller quantities of sea salt.)

6. Do I eat too much fat? There may be many arguments as to which is better for you — vegetable oils or dairy fats — and there is no real doubt at all that too much fat of any sort is harmful. My advice is to cut down your total fat intake, make sure that any meat you eat is lean, and that you balance your consumption of fats between a little animal and dairy on the one hand and a majority of vegeta-ble oils that are rich in polyunsaturates on the other. More than forty per cent of many people's total daily calorie intake is derived from fats, and this should be reduced as NACNE recommends to a maximum of thirty per cent.

Right, as you are determined to eat for health, now for slimming the cider vinegar way!

THREE RULES

First rule:

Start off your day by *sipping* two teaspoonsful of cider vinegar in a tumbler of cold or lukewarm water. Have it ready by the side of your bed.

Second rule:

Sip a tumbler of water containing the two teaspoonsful of cider vinegar *during* each of the three main meals of the day — breakfast, lunch and dinner. Try to make your drink last the whole meal through. If you cut out any meal, have the cider vinegar drink instead.

Third rule:

Chew your food thoroughly. This is to give the cider vinegar the greatest chance to act.

If you are fat or even a bit overweight, this change in your body did not happen in a week or two. You have grown larger gradually, perhaps over many years. *WARNING! Do not reduce too fast.* If you rush it, not only will your skin sag but you will become overtired and fractious.

Achieving the right weight is a wonderful thing to do. Be happy whilst you slim. This really is possible when you slim with cider vinegar.

Now for some experiences of those who have succeeded and now make cider vinegar a part of their daily routine:

Mrs E.D., an old age pensioner from Shrewsbury writes:
'I have taken 2 tsp. of cider vinegar with each meal for 8-9 months, not bothering when out or looking after guests. Last month I lost another 2 lb. making 17 lb. over the period.'

Mrs M.D., of Perthshire, Scotland says:
'I have been taking cider vinegar daily for six months and have lost 21 pounds.'

It was Miss J.B. of Ripon, who said:
'Cider vinegar is a girth's best friend!'

This is an amusing truth which applies not only to girls but also to men. For example, Mr C.F-G., of Glamorgan, found he not only lost weight but improved in general health. A male nurse, Mr C.F., of Bournemouth, found the answer to be cider vinegar, after a long battle with obesity. Mr J.S. of Belfast, was embarrassed by his 'pot' when he went swimming but now he looks fine again.

As long as you keep the THREE RULES you can confidently expect to slim, if you reform your diet, and cider vinegar helps you do this.

Miss S.B., of London, S.E.3, found that she could slim *without* that most difficult attribute — willpower! Mr A.H.E., of Frinton-on-Sea, said that cider vinegar worked wonders for him without any exercise at all, although our view is that slimming comes with cider vinegar but a good shape from a mixture of heredity and exercise. If you were born with a tendency to podgy thighs there is always the possibility that when you slim enough to have gorgeous thighs, you will have a skinny neck or hollow cheeks. Slow slimming, the cider vinegar way, minimizes these problems, whereas rapid slimming aggravates them.

An extra bonus was pointed out by Mrs M.P., of Chesterfield, when she remarked that she had tried dozens of slimming methods without success but when she used the cider vinegar way it not only worked, it was economical. She was supported by very many others, including Mrs G.F., of Kings Norton, who said that cider vinegar lost weight for her without any diet at all, but it is most likely that unknown to her, cider vinegar reduced her appetite but kept her feeling full.

In this connection Mrs G.F. is not quite right. You see, we are all on a diet. The problem is whether or not it is the right diet. It is not wise to generalize because human needs are a very personal thing. But one thing is certain, in many, many peoples' diet, cider vinegar is very effective indeed for the normalization of weight. So, if that is your problem, start right away.

ARTHRITIS AND RHEUMATISM

Arthritis

A friend's interest in the cider vinegar therapy for arthritis was awakened many years ago when he found that one of his thumbs had suddenly become so weak that he could not lift a jug or dinner plate. The Royal National Orthopaedic Hospital took X-rays and removed much blood for blood tests. The diagnosis was osteo-arthritis. A 'natural cocktail' — a tumbler of warm water in which were dissolved two teaspoonsful each of cider vinegar and molasses and one of pure unblended honey was tried. Within three months he was better and has not had a recurrence since. Spontaneous remissions are always possible. But a spontaneous remission is likely to be the result of the body winning a fight against disease, not just luck.

There are people who do not get on with this mixture. They find cider vinegar alone or cider vinegar and honey the best for them. Others just use crude black molasses with good results, yet others fail to obtain relief but experience among arthritics shows they are a minority when they supplement the cider vinegar and molasses with substances that assist the immune system such as the micro-nutrient selenium, vitamins A, C and E and also natural beta-carotene. Evening primrose oil and marine oils are also valuable and scientifically tested.

The first point to remember is that if there has been a great change in the bone through calcium deposits caused by arthritis, then it is not at all likely that this will be altered. The second thing to remember is that 'a cure' is too much to hope for or to expect.

Look for control of symptoms, easing of pain and a reduction in the development of the condition. Keep as mobile as possible and above all do not give up hope. The longer you have had arthritis, the longer it is likely to be before you obtain a helpful result.

Charles Walker, an old friend of mine, related how, when he owned a Health Store in Birkenhead, an elderly man came in one day and danced around the shop. When questioned, he said he was not going crazy, he was demonstrating that he *could* dance. Two years before he had visited the store in a wheel-chair, crippled with arthritis. He had taken cider vinegar and molasses for two years and felt ten years younger! Not everyone can expect such results, but they are at least a matter of common experience.

Dr Jarvis recommends for arthritis:

1. Two teaspoonsful cider vinegar and two of honey in a glass of water, taken at each meal, or if not acceptable, between meals.
2. On Monday, Wednesday and Friday add one drop of iodine at one meal to the mixture.
3. One kelp tablet at breakfast or at all three meals.
4. Avoidance of wheat foods and cereals, white sugar, citrus fruits, muscle meats such as beef, lamb and pork, as these produce an adverse reaction.

He says this regime helps rheumatoid arthritis, osteo-arthritis, bursitis and gout.

We have no quarrel with these procedures but wonder if the dietary restrictions in fact make much difference. As you will have read, we believe that the addition of molasses helps because of the great cleansing power of that food, so our recommendation for arthritis is:

1. On rising, two teaspoonsful of cider vinegar in a tumbler of water.
2. With each meal, two teaspoonsful each of cider vinegar and molasses with one of honey, sipped during the meal in a tumbler of water.
3. A natural vitamin and mineral supplement each day. (See preceding page)
4. A diet very low in sugar and refined flour.
5. A diet low in animal fat.

Mrs D.T. of Pinner, who has a spine that has had to be surgically fixed together, is now free from pain by following this treatment. After years of pain she finds the feeling of relief unbelievable.

Mr F.N. of Willenhall writes: 'not only has cider vinegar, honey and molasses helped my arthritis but for general health it is so good that people ask me where I get my energy from (I am 80 years old).'

Mr J.J. of Edinburgh says that he no longer requires the use of drugs or a collar since taking cider vinegar alone.

Mrs F.S. of London, S.E.11, found that although she is almost crippled with arthritis, cider vinegar was a great help in keeping it under control.

Mrs M.S. of Rotherham found that mixing cider vinegar with honey brought her quick relief, whereas Mrs M.H. of Tuffley found that cider vinegar with molasses gave her the most effective relief from pain.

Mrs E.H. of Winchester writes: 'I have been an addict of cider vinegar since buying a Cyril Scott book many years ago. I have recommended the product to many friends especially sufferers from arthritis. My husband and I are approaching eighty years of age and neither of us have a twinge, and enjoy perfect health. We play bowls and do modern sequence dancing several times a week. My husband drinks his cider vinegar with lunch — calling it his dry white wine!'

When a doctor uses modern drugs in the treatment of arthritis he is involved with many problems such as controlling the side-effects of cortisone or the gastric problems of aspirin. And then there were the terrible problems associated with the use of Opren. You have none of these difficulties when employing the cider vinegar method, although it must be stated that in intractable cases the whole armoury of medicine in skilled hands is needed to make life tolerable for some of those who suffer from serious arthritis.

Do try to start treatment early on. In this way you may much delay or permanently avoid the development of more serious symptoms and control your condition through safe and natural means.

Muscular Rheumatism

This is a muscular condition which may be caused by the build-up of poisons in the muscles or by the failure of the body to remove toxic wastes quickly enough. In general it has been found that treatment as for arthritis is usually helpful. It must be pointed out though that they are not the same, as arthritis affects joints and rheumatism the muscles. It tends to be aggravated by draughts and damp clothes.

Ordinary muscular rheumatism is sometimes not all that serious, especially if you look after yourself, avoiding excessive exertions to which you are not accustomed.

Mrs A.P. of Cardiff tells us that with cider vinegar alone she has had great relief from her muscular rheumatism.

Mrs K.M.C., who found great benefit for her condition, said she was told of it by a very old lady who had known the remedy for 80 years!

Mr J.M.N. of Barnstaple was suffering frequently and now takes a dessertspoonful each of honey and cider vinegar in water so that it has become a way of life — without any more aches and pains. He goes on to say that his favourite cider vinegar is so mellow, mature and smooth tasting that it can be taken like wine without offending the stomach.

Gout

Although gout is often associated with rheumatism in people's minds, it is likely that it is somewhat different in cause. Modern medicines relieve the acutely painful attack in a way no natural remedy can.

The cider vinegar, honey and molasses mixture is, in case of gout, best taken half as strong and twice as often so that you have a pint of the weaker liquid at each meal.

Avoid port and red wine. (Pitt, the statesman, had gout at twenty-one but is usually a problem of middle age). Eat little muscle meat, no sardines or roe. Plenty of wholegrain foods and fresh fruit. If you really have to drink alcohol, whisky and water appears to be statistically preferable for there is a very low incidence of gout in Scotland.

NOSE AND THROAT DISORDERS

Colds

Not only does the common cold and its complications cause a great deal of time to be taken from work, it also usually makes the sufferer a misery to himself and a threat to others.

Professor Linus Pauling of the U.S.A. has written of the good effects of very large doses of vitamin C in the prevention and treatment of colds. This theory has been supported by trials in British and Canadian universities and at the Cold Research Unit on Salisbury Plain, especially when taken at the very earliest signs of an infection. Although the long-term physical effects of these large doses are not yet finally established and could cause kidney stones after prolonged usage in a few susceptible people, Professor Pauling believes that we all need more vitamin C than is customary and suggests we keep it on the table in powder form to sprinkle over our food and put into drinks. 1,000 milligrams (1 gram) of vitamin C a day is very helpful but when exposed to colds or at the beginning of one, increase the dose to 1 gram every three hours. This can, with great advantage, be taken in the cider vinegar drink.

The vitamin C therapy does not work with everyone. An American put on a play in London some time ago and the producer wished to avoid, as it was a winter opening, the problem of having colds among the cast. An actor who appeared in the show told me that in spite of injections of vitamin C, plus large daily doses of tablets, this was the only play he has ever appeared in which had to close down for several nights because of the epidemic of colds among cast and understudies alike! But it does work for most people, especially with cider vinegar, at least to minimize the symptoms. For others cider vinegar alone reduces the number of colds, probably by building up the general bodily resistance.

Several observers believe that natural vitamin C, which contains the bioflavonoids usually present in nature, is far more effective than pure chemical vitamin C, so if you are not having success with the cheaper synthetic product then try some of the excellent natural preparations you can find in health stores.

Coughs

If you have a mild cough it is a good idea to have a glass of double strength cider vinegar drink, that is, four teaspoonsful of cider vinegar to a glass of water. Swallow a few sips slowly when the cough is aggravating. This often brings relief and at night permits sleep.

Mr T.B. of Hailsham has rid himself of night cough after many months by means of this treatment.

Laryngitis

Cyril Scott recommends as an effective treatment, one teaspoonful of the cider vinegar to half a glass of water every hour for seven hours. It is also a valuable precautionary measure when you are exposed to infection. A little honey added to the mixture is most helpful.

Sore Throat

The bacteria often responsible for sore throats prefer an alkaline environment and this may be the reason why the same treatment as for laryngitis works well. If the throat is sore or relaxed after too much talking and especially if you have to address a group of people or you are going to appear in public to talk, perhaps about health, and your voice is hardly above a whisper, you will find it essential to have a first-aid method of avoiding embarrassment even if only for a short time. The first-aid is a special gargle which usually gives instant relief that is usually maintained for up to three-quarters of an hour. To make it, take:

Special Gargle for the Throat

    10 fl oz (275ml) cider vinegar
    4 oz (100g) honey
    1 oz (25g) red sage (garden sage, *Salvia officinalis*)
    ½ oz (15g) self-heal (*Prunella vulgaris*)

Heat the cider vinegar with the herbs until it is almost, but not quite, boiling. (Make sure that the pan is *not* enamelled iron or aluminium.) Allow to cool slowly. Strain after twenty-four hours, add the honey, stir until dissolved, bottle and cap securely. Use two teaspoonsful in half a glass of water.

Catarrh

Many users have found cider vinegar to assist the clearance of catarrh. Take the basic drink of two teaspoonsful in a glass of water three times daily but, in addition, put a couple of inches of pure cider vinegar in a small stainless steel or enamel saucepan, simmer it gently and inhale the vapours for five or ten minutes. This procedure brings relief which often lasts up to eight hours.

Nose Bleeding
Because cider vinegar is an astringent it is worth trying the same way as for catarrh in cases of persistent nose bleeding.

NERVES, CHOKING NERVOUS COUGH
The helpful effects of cider vinegar in many cases of insomnia due to tension are well recognized but an extension of this use as a relaxing beverage came to our notice recently and we cannot do better than quote from the letter written by Miss L.E.B. of Edinburgh:

'I would like to give you an unsolicited testimonial for cider vinegar, for it has literally given me a new lease of life. Although I had been on a course of molasses for six years, I thought I would start taking cider apple vinegar with my main meal.

For 30 years I have never had a single meal without CHOKING and going blue in the face. My throat would just close right up. Sometimes I could manage half-way through a meal, but it always ended up the same. Consequently, I lost friends, people stopped asking me out and I was a nuisance to myself and everyone else. During the war in the services I had to stand by and see someone else eating my rations because I could not swallow.

One night about a year and a half ago, I was sitting alone and eating my evening meal when it suddenly came to me *I was not choking any more*! I can never tell you what this meant to me — catch *me* going on a diet! Ever since, if I take two teaspoonsful in water with meals, I can eat everything that is put in front of me. In fact I like my food better if I take the vinegar with it — I can go anywhere, cafes, other people's homes. I have joined a Burn's Club and we have gone all over the place during the past 12 months and I have had no trouble at all. Perhaps, if you know of other sufferers like myself, recommend cider vinegar. The doctor said it was nerves but thanks to cider vinegar all is now well and I am making up for lost time.'

This very interesting report does demonstrate the profound balancing and normalizing effect of cider vinegar in a most human situation. When you are afflicted by nerves and tensions try not to resort to habit-forming and mentally exhausting drugs such as the tranquillizers. They are the cause of increasing national and international concern for, while they are a blessing to some who are suffering extreme pressures or tensions, they are too freely given in cases where a natural remedy, such as cider vinegar, will give relief without risk of any sort. There are also many herbal products that are most effective.

INSOMNIA

This section is about ordinary sleeplessness not resulting from pain or illness. Drugs do not usually *cure* insomnia. They just desensitize the mind for a while, often leaving a 'hang-over' next morning. We have written of the dangers of the indiscriminate use of powerful habit-forming drugs.

Good sleep is nature's great restorative. Some people, such as Margaret Thatcher, are able to make do with three or four hours each night. For most of us, though, it occupies about one-third of our entire lives, so we had best learn to do it well.

The effects of sleep are felt on the majority of our bodily functions. The first sign is a deepening of the breathing and a slowing of the heart beat. The blood pressure falls. The body temperature drops by about half a Fahrenheit degree (or a quarter Centigrade). Your feet grow warmer and your hands colder. The sweat glands are very busy, so good ventilation is necessary. The blood supply to the brain does not decrease. Indeed, your brain is active at night. About an hour after you fall asleep, the pupils of your eyes move quite rapidly. This movement appears to be an essential component of really refreshing sleep and its onset and duration is delayed if sedative drugs are used.

What then can we learn from all this to help our slumbers? Firstly as night approaches, you must cultivate quite consciously a peaceful frame of mind. Think of good things and nice people. Some gentle music often helps. It will be good if you have taken a little exercise in the open air — a short walk, perhaps, brisk enough to tire you a little. Remember that people need differing amounts of sleep although this is inconvenient if your marriage partner needs twice (or half) as much as you do!

In any case, as you grow older you tend to need *less* sleep.

Next it is good to have a warm nourishing drink half-an-hour before retiring. Just before going to bed sip half a tumblerful of cider vinegar and honey, 2 teaspoonsful of each in warm water. Lie down, think pleasant thoughts, relax your body, starting at the toes and going right through the frame until the fingertips are relaxed — breathe deeply and regularly. Do not be worried about *not* sleeping — do not be worried about anything at all — there is nothing you can do to change things in the middle of the night anyway.

Make sure your bedroom is warm enough. Breathing very cold or damp air is bad for the chest and aggravates bronchitis, especially amongst senior citizens. They have, too, a peculiar problem. As the kidneys age, the water they pass to the bladder becomes less and less strong, so there is more of it! Drinking less is quite the worst thing to do. Your kidneys *need* the water to carry on the process of excretion. Just resign yourself to maybe having to rise a couple of times in the night. Take a few more sips of the honey/cider vinegar combination and go peacefully back to sleep again. Many older people read a book in the night or do a few little chores. Just make sure, when you leave your bed, that you do not become chilled.

If you cannot sleep because of pain, grief or illness, then you may need the care and advice of a qualified practitioner who is in a position to advise you upon your individual needs.

ASTHMA

In times past this used to be called the Devil's Disease. Happily, the majority of sufferers are now able to obtain relief from the worst symptoms and often, when the cause is an allergy, a complete cure. Yet others have a spontaneous cessation, or it may be supplanted by hay fever. On the other hand, asthma, although it is most common amongst children and young adults, sometimes does not appear until the forties.

During an attack the person has a feeling of tightness in the throat and neck with perhaps a frightening feeling of suffocation. Breathing is difficult, especially breathing out. Sticky mucus, which later becomes thin, is coughed up. The attack usually ends with a feeling of extreme tiredness.

It is caused by a sudden reduction in diameter of the small tubes in the lungs combined with the production of a lot of mucus. The patient wheezes because of the difficulty of forcing air out through these narrow tubes.

Why the tubes become narrow is a more difficult question. There are three recognized reasons: firstly, an attack of bronchitis sometimes starts asthma off; secondly, asthma can be an allergic reaction to a particular pollen or types of dust, for example, or to certain food additives such as the yellow colour tartrazine (E102) and the preservative sulphites

(E220); thirdly, it can be inherited from forbears with asthma or hay fever or nettle rash.

The cider vinegar treatment with honey (2 teaspoonsful of each in a tumbler of water thrice daily) has produced some remarkable results. It is certainly worth trying but also it is important for the sufferer to avoid aggravating his own condition by adopting a life as free as possible from stresses and strains and by not placing himself in the way of any causative factors which experience has previously indicated. Smoking is best abandoned. Fatness, or even slight overweight, throws an excessive strain onto the body during an attack, so slim! Happily, an asthmatic lady usually avoids attacks when expecting a child. Try eating as natural a diet, organically grown is best, as you can. Sometimes milk and chocolate are best avoided for a trial period to see if they are part of the problem.

Mr M. McK. of Suffolk 'cured' his long-standing asthma by cider vinegar in water *without* honey, but as most of the experiments have been done with honey, that should be the first preference.

HAY FEVER

The sufferer has what appears to be a very bad summer cold, but there is no infection. Hay fever is caused by sensitization to proteins. We all tend to reject protein of a sort different to our own, that is why tissue transplants are so difficult to carry out effectively. The air is full of pollen protein on a hot summer's day to which many people are acutely sensitive. They pray for rain to keep the pollen count to a bearable level.

Special nasal sprays are sometimes used but these often cause permanent damage to the delicate lining of the nose.

Hay fever is rare in very small infants and almost unknown in the first year. It tends to reduce in intensity as middle age approaches although it does not often go entirely. Be very careful not to feed baby solid foods, especially those containing wheat, too early. If possible wait 4-6 months so transferring the maximum protection from the mother's milk to the child.

An exception, which is an example well worth following, is Mrs L.E.G. of Thorpe Bay, who obtained a complete cure by taking, once a day throughout the season, 2 teaspoonsful each of honey and cider vinegar in a glassful of water and, at the same time, cutting out all sugar.

When she wrote she had been fine for eleven years, having been a very bad sufferer for the previous thirty-four years. Her experience was published in the *Sunday Express*. She subsequently received no less than 4,000 letters and replied to each one! This at least must recommend the therapy! Many of those who tried the method were as successful as she, others were not, but in any case general health and resistance will have been improved.

Miss C.J.P. of Southend-on-Sea writes:

'I recommend cider vinegar to my friends with hay fever, rheumatism, etc. During last summer's hay fever season I stopped people in the street in Southend High Street telling them about the cider vinegar and honey mixture whenever I saw anyone sneezing obviously from hay fever. Following the discussion on the BBC "You and Yours" programme about hay fever I wrote to them telling them that cider vinegar and honey kept me free this summer. Two days later my letter was read out on this programme. Since thousands must listen to the programme I would imagine many hay fever sufferers are now taking the mixture as I suggested — that is one dose at night all the year round.'

BEAUTY

The skin, like the eyes, is one of the most obvious places to look for signs of tiredness, age, worry or poor general health. Healthy skin has a bloom and elasticity which, with care, lasts into old age. I do not believe that cider vinegar will bring about a miraculous transformation but those who take it in the usual way for other purposes frequently report a great general improvement in skin tone and appearance which causes them to continue with regular doses.

The reason may lie in the inner cleanliness which is a feature of the treatment. Yellowing eyes are a sign of 'liverishness' and in mild cases cider vinegar taken internally is a great help.

Hair is dead except at the point of growth in the hair follicle but to remain in the best condition it is important to give the scalp a favourable environment.

It happens that shampoo is usually alkaline. The scalp, on the other hand, is acid and protected by natural fats. Nature's protection is washed away allowing skin to become scaly and the scalp dry. The balance can be restored by using a cider vinegar rinse after you have shampooed your hair. Many hair stylists use this rinse in preference to the well-known beer rinse because they prefer the cosmetic result. When you add to this the benefit of the treatment to the condition of the scalp, you have discovered a reason why so many use cider vinegar externally as well as internally.

There are several ways of using cider vinegar as a beauty treatment, but as few users would wish to smell with an odour more reminiscent of a fish and chip shop than a beauty parlour it is a good plan to make a pleasant infusion. A favourite is:

Rosemary and Cider Vinegar Skin Lotion

Place 1 oz (25g) of fresh rosemary or ½ oz (15g) dried rosemary in a saucepan with half-a-pint (275ml) of water (rain water is best). Bring slowly to the boil, simmer gently for ten minutes, strain, mix with half-a-pint of cider vinegar. When cool, pour in bottles that can be securely sealed. Store in a dark, cool place.

This makes a fine general purpose lotion. If you wish, by all means add a few drops of eau de Cologne or perfume. Also other herbs can be used or rose petals even, but rosemary is good for the hair.

You can use the lotion in the following ways:

For a Hair Conditioner — A little poured into the palms of the hands, rubbed vigorously into the scalp with the finger tips.

For a Hair Rinse — A tablespoonful in the final rinsing water makes a wonderful cosmetic rinse.

For the Skin — Dab the lotion on the face very gently, working out from the wrinkles and sagging places.

For Swellings — Some remarkable results are achieved with this lotion or, in fact, just plain cider vinegar, in cases of swellings caused by fatigue, long standing or strained muscles. Apply liberally every hour until the swelling reduces. If you can, make a cold compress from the lotion. This has a very good effect on severe strains. Many people's feet and legs swell whilst travelling. The cider vinegar treatment, both internally and externally, is a valuable aid.

VARICOSE VEINS

These must be cared for by a properly qualified person but they are, nevertheless, often most uncomfortable. As Mrs V.M. of Huddersfield wrote: 'Cider Vinegar gives me great relief from varicose veins.' The treatment cannot be considered in any way a cure but has a beneficial effect nonetheless. For small varicose veins, calendula cream is very good.

FINGER-NAILS

A doctor can often tell much from an examination of the nails. The white spots which sometimes appear are generally due to a deficiency of calcium. It is a frequent observation that these spots disappear when cider vinegar is being used. This is not because it is a provider of calcium in large amounts, although an appreciable proportion is present, but because it helps the body to make more effective use of the calcium in the diet.

Growing children need more calcium than adults and usually obtain it from milk. Older people, on the other hand, find efficient use of sufficient calcium a help in preserving strong bones and in mending them following a fracture.

The nails, then, can show the effects of the cider vinegar treatment in the elimination of white spots. At the same time, some users have reported a general strengthening of thin and brittle nails. Mrs M.M. of Kingsbury, who was a sufferer from generally weak nails, found relief for the first time after many unsuccessful experiments and her nails are now completely restored. This cannot take place overnight — even a year may be needed before results are apparent, especially with older sufferers from weak nails.

EYES

We have mentioned the better appearance of the eyes frequently noticed as an effect of the treatment. So often we find the physical outward attributes of a user improve as a direct result of the internal benefit of cider vinegar.

Mr E.A.K. of Portsmouth, reports that he found that a cataract which was forming in one of his eyes stopped progressing so rapidly as before when he took cider vinegar regularly. On the other hand, it must be confessed that this is not a common finding, although not unique, and it may have been a spontaneous slowing-down. So take opthalmic or medical advice if you have an eye problem.

SHINGLES

This is caused by the same virus as chicken pox as parents who have never had chicken pox sometimes find to their anguish when infected by their children. It causes burning pain usually along the path of a nerve. The pain is generally gone with the rash after about a week but occasionally persists. Sufferers, such as Mr W.C.F. of Lancing, have found neat cider vinegar dabbed regularly upon the sore areas to give far more relief than any medicament. The pain abates quite soon after each treatment but returns after an hour or so, when the application needs to be repeated.

THE DIGESTION

Many digestive orders arise from a relatively small number of defects. Sometimes the bacteria which work to break down our food for us are of the wrong kind. The problem of too much acidity is not as common as the sellers of patent alkaline medicines may have you believe. In fact, the *reverse* is often true — sufferers from indigestion may not have enough acid.

When you eat food it goes through a first process of digestion in the mouth where the starches are turned, during the chewing process, into sugar by the enzymes in the saliva. Because chewing helps to break down the food and stimulate the flow of saliva it is important to chew thoroughly. Many of those who live on grain diets, and Eastern philosophers, say chewing each mouthful forty times produces the best results. For our part, we become rather bored a long time before that!

The human saliva is usually alkaline but the active enzyme works best in a slightly acid medium, so we have found our first indication of the value of the cider vinegar drink in that it assists the maintenance of the desired acidity.

After the food has been formed into a conveniently sized portion you swallow it and it descends the eight or nine inches to the stomach which is a collecting sack for the food you eat. The digestive process now carries on a further stage in the stomach. The gastric juices contain about 0.4 per cent of free hydrochloric acid together with enzymes which make the food liquid. Harmful bacteria and other organisms are usually made harmless whilst the food is in the stomach.

Digestion and absorption of the nutrients continues in the twenty-two feet long small intestine where there are more enzymes and a lot of valuable and essential bacteria which help to break down food into substances which can be absorbed by the body.

These bacteria appear to find, as animal results have shown, much benefit from cider vinegar. One theory, mentioned elsewhere, is that because cider vinegar contains both a high potassium content and acetic acid in apparently balanced amounts, the body is able to convert these raw materials in an entirely natural way into a substance which checks the growth of unwelcome bacteria, allowing the useful types to become more vigorous. There is at present no scientific work to confirm or deny this theory but such research certainly needs funding.

Water is absorbed into the body in the four feet of large intestine where waste matter is accumulated, prior to elimination.

Research by distinguished doctors, including a Fellow of the Royal Society, Dr Denis Burkitt, and his colleague the surgeon, Mr Neil Painter, has shown beyond reasonable doubt that for a really healthy digestive system it is necessary to have a quantity of cereal or vegetable fibre daily. The simplest way of taking this is to consume two level dessertspoons of bran each day. This can be mixed with a little of the cider vinegar drink or added to your food. The results are remarkable provided the bran treatment is carried on indefinitely. As with all nutritional guidelines, do not fall into the trap of thinking that if you take far more you will be even healthier. A varied and balanced diet is best for most of us.

Having taken care of the general condition of your digestive organs, the specific effects of cider vinegar are themselves of interest and value.

Indigestion

As Mrs D.A. of Folkestone says, 'Until I took a glassful of cider vinegar drink with each meal I did not know what it was to experience a meal free from pain and subsequent discomfort.'

Mrs A.W. of Monmouth suffered from flatulence especially when eating pastry. She found complete relief by adding one teaspoonful of the vinegar to her pastry mix.

Mr R.E. actually suffered from indigestion due to acidity yet found a daily cider vinegar drink, in spite of being itself acid, an effective answer.

After excessive or unwise eating or drinking the high potassium content is probably a factor in the settling effect obtained by taking the cider vinegar drink. Miss K.S. went on further when she said that she found cider vinegar allowed indulgence without indigestion!

Constipation

This distressing condition cannot be good for you because of the pressures created in the intestine when 'forcing' is necessary. I have said that bran is an essential part of treatment, but cider vinegar is also a great help.

Laxatives are not very good for you, besides being expensive, so try a glassful of water containing 2 teaspoonsful of cider vinegar on rising, during the main meal of the day and before retiring. If this, plus two tablespoonsful of bran each day does not solve your problem try yogurt or some special fruit cubes from Belgium (Orfisan) from health stores. If after a month you are still suffering then we would advise your seeking qualified help and advice.

Diarrhoea

If diarrhoea alternates with constipation you must seek medical assistance, for it is just possible that this is an early warning that all is not well with your gut.

Strawberries affect some people, so do travelling, emotional disturbance and certain conditions or illnesses. The cure is to rectify the cause where this is possible. On the other hand, most diarrhoea is an unfortunate and temporary inconvenience for which cider vinegar is a good first-aid treatment. As one result of diarrhoea is the elimination of much of the water that is usually absorbed by the large intestine, you need plenty of fluids, two or three *extra* pints a day. Add *one* teaspoonful of the vinegar to each half pint (275ml). Sometimes a kaolin mixture, B.P.C., helps, but the consensus of opinion in simple cases not associated with illness is against most of the travellers' preventive tablets containing clioquinol sold by chemists because of the occasional side-effects.

If an infection is the cause of the problem then you must have the infection treated. The cider vinegar drink can safely be taken in addition to any treatment that is prescribed. Drink plenty of fluids to avoid dehydration. Add salts in the tropics.

Hiccoughs

This occurs when your diaphragm is not synchronized properly with the flap which prevents you swallowing air into the stomach. It can arise from a variety of causes.

Normally it goes away within the hour, unless it is due to some more serious condition, when the underlying cause should be located and treated. Hiccoughs can be tiring, so it is usual to seek aid if it persists for more than four hours.

The cider vinegar first-aid treatment is to sip, very slowly a teaspoonful of undiluted cider vinegar whilst plugging the ears with the fingers (it takes two to achieve this!). This usually brings about an immediate cure. If not, try breathing in and out of a *paper* bag for a minute or two. This creates carbon dioxide which stimulates the breathing centre.

Heartburn
A burning sensation behind the breastbone an hour or so after meals is often found to diminish or vanish when cider vinegar is taken with the meal.

HEART CONDITIONS
Heart disease is the main killer of people in the prime of life. Men are vulnerable after the age of thirty-five. Women are usually not likely to have an attack until after the 'change', although the rate is rising, especially for women 'on the pill'.

There is no single cause of this curse of Western civilization, which is only rarely encountered amongst those who live on a natural unprocessed diet, but prevention is easier than cure. Perhaps we know half the causes, so to keep to the rules substantially reduces your risk.

Rules to avoid Heart Attacks
1. If you are not slim, become slim (see section on slimming).
2. Avoid excessive sugar and foods made with much added sugar.
3. Avoid hard fats such as animal fat, coconut and palm oils. Replace them with unsaturated soft fats, such as sunflower seed oil, safflower, soya, corn, olive and fish oils. Cut down total fat intake.
4. Take enough exercise to become gently breathless each day; walk upstairs instead of using the lift.
5. Give up smoking.
6. Avoid constipation by taking bran and cider vinegar (see page 40). Sometimes older people temporarily increase blood pressure through straining, with fatal results.
7. Keep work, recreation, rest and holidays in a sensible balance, after all if you literally work yourself to death you will not be of much use to your family or community.
8. Eat a balanced, mixed diet, taking care not to overcook vegetables or to use too much water.
9. Avoid excessive salt (sodium chloride), the element sodium *in excess* increases the tendency of some people to high blood pressure. Use a little sea salt.
10. Try to have several small meals each day, not one huge feast which

could throw a strain onto the body by increasing greatly the amount of fat in the blood stream.

11. Take a balanced multivitamin, as well as mineral and trace elements as food supplements to ensure a daily sufficiency. Megadoses are strictly for use under expert guidance only.

From the foregoing it is plain that cider vinegar cannot be claimed to prevent, or for that matter to cure, heart troubles or allied disorders. Nevertheless, it can play a part in helping you to achieve or maintain the right weight. Additionally, some individuals find it does give them relief from certain symptoms.

Angina

Angina is a condition in which the arteries of the heart do not always pass enough blood. This gives rise to a sometimes suffocating pain in the upper chest which often also affects the left arm and the neck. This is similar to the type of pain often occurring in a coronary heart attack but, with rest, it passes off. Doctors give nitroglycerin tablets which must be chewed and give almost immediate relief. Patients who look after themselves have a good outlook and future.

Mr R.R. of Kemsing found the cider vinegar drink taken regularly lessened the severity of the attack. But you may agree with Mr E.J. of Blackpool, who, as a sufferer, takes the cider vinegar treatment in order to keep his weight down and so improve his anginal condition.

HIGH BLOOD PRESSURE

This is also called hypertension. Sufferers benefit considerably by adopting the eleven rules for avoiding heart attacks.

In their own cases, Mrs C.W. of Huddersfield and Mrs F.W. of Newtown found that the cider vinegar drink three times daily helped keep blood pressure down. This is likely to be because of an improvement in their general condition through the treatment.

CRAMP

Cramp is quite common amongst the middle-aged and elderly. It may arise because the muscles suffer from a building up of poisonous wastes which the circulation does not take away with enough speed. A number of sufferers have told us that the cider drink, preferably with honey in warm water, taken before retiring, reduces the frequency of attacks.

BURNS

Use pure, undiluted cider vinegar straight from the bottle to relieve the pain and soreness of minor burns.

Modern treatment for burns advocates very rapid cooling with lots of cold water as soon as a burn occurs. This is also vital when clothes are either burnt or wettened with a hot liquid. Pour cold water over the clothes at once. If it is a bad burn, always summon medical aid. Keep the patient warm and rested with something to drink. Do not remove clothing from, or otherwise disturb, the burnt area. Minor burns benefit from the cider vinegar treatment. When possible, it is best to leave them exposed to the air, provided that the skin is intact.

SUNBURN

The same general rules apply here as for ordinary burns. The cider vinegar dabbed on is most soothing. Really serious cases require medical help. Although cider vinegar is very good for treating sunburn, it is in no sense a preventive. A properly prepared filtering oil or lotion and a good deal of caution are both needed for a really happy holiday in the sun. Natural beta-carotene taken for 4 weeks prior to exposure helps build up your protective mechanisms.

TEETH AND MOUTH

Cyril Scott, who still had a good few teeth in his nineties, recommended the use of cider vinegar, one teaspoon in water night and morning, as a mouth wash. He said that the teeth should be brushed with the solution and that cider vinegar drinkers had unusually white teeth.

Scott mentioned that two tablespoonsful of the vinegar to a kettle of water which is allowed to stand for a time allows the lime deposits to come away when the water is poured off, or it can be more easily scraped away without damaging the inner surface of the kettle.

Mouth ulcers and sores also benefit from the mouth wash; and for a tendency towards bleeding gums the mouth wash is helpful in addition to the cider vinegar treatment three times a day.

Chapter 5

CIDER VINEGAR IN THE KITCHEN

If you are convinced of the health advantages of cider vinegar, then the logical next step is to enjoy it as much as possible. The kitchen offers many delectable opportunities to use cider vinegar in ways which are a complement to your good taste.

The chef of one of the most distinguished hotels in London renowned for its cuisine, uses cider vinegar for its flavour in preference to wine or malt vinegar.

You should, in any case, as a general rule, eat whole foods that are as free as possible from any chemical additives, which still permits gourmet cooking. Start the family on choosing tasty but good and varied foods from childhood. As soon as they can read they can join in reading the labels when you go shopping to see if prepared foods are also, as many are, made from the sort of ingredients you would wish to use at home.

This will set a sure foundation for sound health so that spells of bad eating due to school or being away from home or with friends can be taken in their stride.

It is necessary to be concerned about what you eat but not worried for there are hardly any *bad* foods if they are eaten as a minor or occasional part of the diet.

This cooking section sets out to let you into some of the delightful and varied uses for cider vinegar in the home. It includes some excellent additional recipes from other well-tried sources which are acknowledged in their due place.

Please remember that cider vinegar does sometimes form 'mother of vinegar' if the cap is not replaced tightly. If you are buying a gallon for economic reasons, it is not necessarily going to keep without some possibility of deterioration for a year or more, as some users expect. Six months is a fair life for a large bottle. Even then it is best to decant the gallon size into very clean half or one pint strongly stoppered bottles if you wish to use it over a longish period.

BASIC VINEGARS

Herbal or spiced vinegars are delightful to 'spike' the flavour of savoury dishes. You can also store herbs for the winter in a far more aromatic state than by drying them (although dry herbs have very many uses) by putting them tightly packed into a jar of cider vinegar. When you need the herb; just shake it dry and use in the way you prefer, or use a little of the vinegar itself.

For the flavoured vinegars it is best to buy sufficient small sized bottles of cider vinegar to provide one for each variety. Be sure to stick an appropriate label on after you have prepared the vinegar. It would be rather a shock to use chilli vinegar as a mouth wash!

Basic Method

The basic methods are similar, except when specified. You remove a little vinegar if necessary, add the appropriate flavouring, re-seal and leave for a few days or a week before using. There is not normally any need to remove the herbs before use, in fact the flavour improves with age. The quantities are right for a 10 to 13 oz (275 to 375ml) bottle.

Celery Vinegar — Chop a ¼lb (100g) of cleaned root and white stalk, leave for a month. Or use ¼oz (7½g) celery seed instead. A pinch of seed is sometimes preferred in the first recipe. Good with salads.

Chilli Vinegar — Use one or two whole hot red or green chillies. One of each is nice. Dried chillies will do, but are not so full of flavour. Wonderful with fish dishes, curries and oysters.

Cucumber Vinegar — Chop 3 oz (75g) of cucumber, including the skin, together with a shallot or small onion with a crushed peppercorn. Very fragrant and refreshing with salads and cold meat.

Fennel Vinegar — Slice two outside leaves of fennel. You can also add some parsley if you like. Good with mutton and fish.

Fines Herbes Vinegar — This is a famous French general purpose flavoured vinegar. Excellent as a basis for a salad dressing. Use one half-teaspoonful each of whole peppercorns, tarragon and basil, the grated skin of a small lemon, a pinch each of savory, thyme, sea salt and raw sugar. One chopped shallot or a little onion, a scrape of dried horseradish, a small pinch of pimento and of crushed chopped bay leaf, one leaf of rosemary. This takes several months but is worth it! If you find this vinegar a little strong, then divide the contents of the first bottle into another.

Garlic Vinegar — The old recipe says that this is best made between Midsummer and Michaelmas, but that was before we could import garlic so easily. Some do not like the smell or flavour. We like both and believe it helps bring out most savoury flavours. Garlic is said to be good for you — never mind what the others say! Peel, chop and add one ounce (25g) of fresh garlic. Shake the bottle each day for ten days, then strain and re-bottle. You need use only a few drops at a time.

Horseradish and Chilli Vinegar — A powerful one, this! Use one ounce (25g) of grated horseradish, a teaspoonful of sea salt, a saltspoonful of dried ginger root, a pinch of cayenne pepper and a whole hot chilli.

Nasturtium Vinegar — Quite a piquant and unusual flavour comes from using a handful of freshly gathered nasturtium flowers, one clove, two peppercorns, a hint of crushed garlic and one chopped shallot (or a little onion). This is best kept for a month or two before using.

Rosemary Vinegar (Italian style) — Use a large sprig each of rosemary and of peppermint, together with a half teaspoonful of chopped angelica root.

Shallot Vinegar — Use 4 oz (100g) of chopped shallots. A large onion will do instead but the flavour is not as good.

Spiced Vinegar — In this case the spices need to be simmered with a very little of the vinegar. This is then added when cool to the rest and allowed to mature for a week. It is best then sieved and re-bottled. Use half a teaspoonful each of crushed chillies, pimento and coriander with a quarter teaspoonful each of cloves, ginger root, mustard powder and black pepper.

Tarragon Vinegar — Known to the French as *estragon*, tarragon is perhaps the most French of all herbs. It is strong, so you do not need to use much. Without doubt tarragon is the best herb to go with chicken but as tarragon vinegar it is used in the finest French dressings. Put a few fresh branches into the vinegar and it is soon ready for use. In this instance it is never a good idea to remove the tarragon as the vinegar drains away as you pour it. If you have no tarragon in your garden grow the variety called True French. Russian tarragon is rather less good.

SALAD DRESSINGS

There are not many attractive undressed things and salads are no exception. The variety you can use is a delight to the palate. The cook has the pleasure of deciding which will suit both the guests and the salad.

Olive oil has a rather heavy and dominating flavour which does not appeal to everyone, but you may certainly use it if you like it. Use a first pressing extra virgin olive oil in that case. Otherwise you will note that we have listed corn oil. This is because it is a good, moderately priced oil without much tendency to rancidity. It has a high content of the valuable unsaturated fats. You can equally well substitute corn oil by soya, safflower or sunflower oils.

Basic French Dressing

    3 parts corn oil
    1 part cider vinegar

Mix and add to the salad just before serving so that every leaf is shining. Many French people would use 6 parts oil to 1 part cider vinegar but that is too oily for some tastes.

Tarragon Dressing

As above, using tarragon cider vinegar instead of the plain sort.

Favourite Dressing

We have evolved this which our guests seem to like — it took a long time to get it right.

At least an hour before the meal (or the day before if you wish) mix:

3 tablespoonsful corn oil
1 tablespoonful cider vinegar
a squeeze of lemon juice
one large crushed clove of garlic (that is one piece from the whole)
a turn of freshly ground black pepper
a teaspoonful of maple syrup or a pinch of raw sugar
a pinch of mustard powder
some mixed herbs (see below)

Add to the salad after a brisk mix either at table or just before serving. Never use so much that there is a lot of free dressing at the bottom of the salad bowl.

For the mixed herbs it is a good idea to keep some assortments of dried herbs in screw-topped jars. Here are two which are slightly different from each other.

Herb Mix (A)

Parsley, tarragon, lemon balm, chervil, chives, dill, thyme, basil.

Herb Mix (B)

Parsley, dill, celery leaf flakes and tarragon.

The herbs are listed in roughly descending order of quantity, first largest, last least.

If you have it, the addition of a splash of walnut oil is aromatic and luxurious.

Yogurt Salad Dressing

This is good as it comes or can have herbs or garlic added as you wish. Blend or whisk thoroughly:

1 small carton of plain yogurt then,
using the carton as a measure
half a carton cider vinegar
half a carton corn oil

Vinaigrette Dressings

These come in a wonderful assortment of flavours. The basic dressing is:

6 tablespoonsful corn oil
2 tablespoonsful cider vinegar
1 teaspoonful chopped capers
1 tablespoonful chopped onion
1 tablespoonful herbs in the mixture, 2 parts parsley to one each of chervil, tarragon and chives.
a pinch of sea salt and pepper.

Mix thoroughly. Use with avocado pears, asparagus, cauliflowers, game, meat or salad. The quantities can be halved or doubled, as required.

Vinaigrette with Eggs

These are two good ways of doings this, the first is best for chicken and fish, the second with salads.

Recipe (A)
Soft boil 2 eggs (3 minutes).
Scoop out the yolks, add these to the basic dressing and mix. Chop the white, stir it gently in.
Recipe (B)
Use 2 hard-boiled chopped eggs, a little chopped gherkin and a little chopped lemon peel with the basic dressing. Stir gently.

Curried Vinaigrette

Add a teaspoonful of curry powder and an extra-finely chopped onion to the basic dressing. Allow to stand several hours before use.

Blue Cheese Dressing

Add from one to four tablespoonsful of crumbled dry Roquefort, Stilton, Danish Blue or Gorgonzola.

Nutty Salad Dressing

This is rather good with cold rice, or with chicory and other full-flavoured salads.

2 tablespoonsful cider vinegar
1 tablespoonful corn oil

¼ teaspoonful mustard powder
1 saltspoonful mixed herbs (see above)
1 egg yolk (raw)
1 tablespoonful mixed coarsley chopped nuts
1 small chopped apple

You need to add the nuts and apple after the other ingredients have been thoroughly beaten together. If you find the dressing a little sharp you can add a touch of honey or of raw sugar to taste.

Banana Dressing
Unusual but an interesting change especially with chicory.

2 tablespoonsful cider vinegar
1 tablespoonful corn oil
1 tablespoonful natural yogurt
a pinch of sea salt and pepper
a big pinch of mixed herbs
1 banana

Crush the banana with a fork until it becomes smooth and creamy. Mix well in firstly the yogurt, then the herbs. Next add the cider vinegar and the oil. Mix very briskly.

You will surely enjoy these cider vinegar dressings and have pleasure discovering and trying many others.

SAUCES
We enjoy the extra fullness of flavour and delicate aroma which comes from using cider vinegar in our sauces. Some of the old, traditional recipes are particularly interesting and much appreciated. A few new ideas bring excitement — but first one of the basic sauces which, although from simple ingredients, requires a little care for good results:

Sauce Hollandaise
This is an occasional rich treat for entertaining or that special dinner and is best made 'finger-tip hot' or just as hot as the finger-tip will stand. Over-heating will produce bad scrambled egg. Take:

8 oz (225g) butter or, preferably polyunsaturated margarine such as Vitaquell or Flora

4 egg yolks
1 tablespoonful cider vinegar
a pinch of sea salt and freshly ground pepper
1 tablespoonful cold water

Boil a large saucepan about one-third full of water. While it is heating, cut the butter or margarine into some twenty small pieces. Put the water, cider vinegar and the egg yolks into a small enamel or stainless steel saucepan, add the salt and pepper and whilst continuing to whisk gently lower the pan into the boiling water.

As soon as the yolks become thicker, take the pan from the water, put in one of the pats of butter. Whisk again to a smooth cream, add another pat of butter. If it melts whisk again to a cream. Go on until the butter does not melt. Return the pan to the water until it just melts again. Do not stop beating. Do this until all the butter has been used. When this has happened again warm-up the sauce, still beating, until it is finger-tip hot. Serve immediately in a warm sauce-boat.

This goes well with the huge tender asparagus spears beloved of the Germans, which are eatable from tip to base — but Hollandaise is good with many vegetables and fish.

Aïoli Sauce

If you believe that garlic is good for you, this sauce is a way of making sure everyone knows. It is made to the consistency of mayonnaise. In Marseille they call if 'Friday Sauce' because it is used on fish. We like it with boiled potatoes, French beans and hard-boiled eggs, as well.

4 cloves garlic (or 2 for each person)
2 egg yolks (or 1 each)
8 fl oz (225ml) corn oil
sea salt, pepper, cider vinegar

Either crush the garlic to a paste or put it in a blender with the egg yolks and salt. Add the oil *very* gradually, whisking or blending all the time. Stop when you have made a thick mayonnaise. Add pepper and cider vinegar to taste. We use about a tablespoon of the vinegar. Lord Burntwood once said that Aïoli was created because of the need to disguise the strong salted fish brought to France by the Newfoundland fishing boats from the eighteenth century onwards.

Mayonnaise

It is possible nowadays to buy ready-made mayonnaise containing cider vinegar, sunflower oil and fresh egg yolks. This is as good as home made, but here is how to do it yourself.

    3 egg yolks
    ½ teaspoonful sea salt
    ½ teaspoonful mustard powder
    1 tablespoonful boiling water
    10 fl oz (275ml) corn or sunflower seed oil
    1 tablespoonful cider vinegar
    (*Tarragon* cider vinegar is best)

Have all the ingredients and the bowl at room temperature. Put egg yolks into the bowl and beat for about a minute until they thicken. Add the cider vinegar, sea salt and mustard. Beat for one more minute. Keep beating steadily and then add the oil a drop at a time. If you go too fast it will curdle. (If that happens start again with another yolk and a little oil and add this to the failure to revive it). As you add more oil it will become easier.

After almost a half has been combined, you can increase the oil to a thin stream. When the oil has been used, beat in a tablespoonful of boiling water. This helps to prevent it separating. Taste to see if you have enough seasoning. Many people find that they prefer two or three tablespoonsful of cider vinegar. If you do this in the blender you need 1 whole egg and 2 yolks.

Having made your mayonnaise, or bought it, you can try lots of good variations.

Louis Sauce (for shellfish)

    6 fl oz (175ml) (about 1 cupful) mayonnaise
    2 tablespoonsful grated onion
    2 fl oz (50ml) chilli sauce (see separate recipe)
    2 tablespoonsful chopped parsley
    3 fl oz (75ml) whipped double cream
    a dash of cayenne

Stir together. Allow to stand for about two hours in a cool place to develop the flavour.

Ravigote Sauce (one of the best for cold vegetables or shellfish)

6 fl oz (175ml) mayonnaise
1 tablespoonful cider vinegar
1 teaspoonful mustard powder
1 chopped shallot
1 tablespoonful chopped capers
1 teaspoonful chopped tarragon

Mix gently. Serve cold.

Thousand Island (the best for prawn cocktail)

6 fl oz (175ml) mayonnaise
1 dash Tabasco sauce or
1 tablespoonful chilli sauce
1 tablespoonful cider vinegar
4 tablespoonsful tomato *purée* (from a tube is easy)

Stir together and chill before use.

Tartare Sauce

6 fl oz (175ml) mayonnaise
1 chopped hard-boiled egg yolk
1 medium-sized grated onion
1 tablespoonful chopped chives
1 teaspoonful fine chopped parsley
1 tablespoonful chopped capers
2 teaspoonsful cider vinegar

Mix well and allow to stand an hour before using.

Mayonnaise Chantilly

6 fl oz (175ml) mayonnaise
2 fl oz (50ml) whipped cream

Stir the two gently together.

You can invent your own. Amongst tried favourites are mayonnaise with any of the following for 6 fl oz (175ml):

Asparagus, 2 oz (50g) chopped, drained

Chives, 1 tablespoonful chopped
Curry powder, 2 teaspoonsful (best if cooked before adding with a little oil and onion)
Cheese (add 3 tablespoonsful grated cheese and some paprika, thin with cream)
Chutney (drain first)
Chilli powder (not too much, ¼ teaspoonful to try)
Green (coloured with juice crushed from 4 tablespoonsful watercress, 2 tablespoonsful parsley)
Mustard (add 2 tablespoonsful mustard powder)
Paprika, 1 teaspoonful (very pretty rose colour)
Verte (pound up 1 teaspoonful chives, 1 tablespoonful chervil, 1 tablespoonful tarragon, 1 tablespoonful spinach with 1 tablespoonful water. Squeeze through muslin into mayonnaise.)

Sauce Béarnaise

This king of French sauces, considered the best accompaniment to steak, but also excellent with many vegetarian dishes and the drier fish, such as cod, swordfish and tuna. The stock should reflect the dish, with vegetable water, fish or meat stock as appropriate.

2 tablespoonsful cider vinegar
1 teaspoonful chopped shallots (or onions)
6 peppercorns
A bay leaf
2 teaspoonsful tarragon
2 teaspoonsful chervil
¼ cupful (approximately) gravy or stock
1½ oz (40g) butter
2 egg yolks

First of all you boil up the shallots and peppercorns, bay leaf, and half of the chervil and tarragon in the cider vinegar until it has reduced to half. Strain and reserve the liquid. Put a double saucepan on and boil it fast (a basin in an ordinary saucepan will do if you give it time to heat through). Mix the egg yolks with a little of the stock and put in the double boiler, stirring constantly. Still stirring, add the butter, a small piece at a time. When the mixture has thickened, add the rest of the stock and then the cider vinegar liquor. Finally, stir in the rest of the chervil and tarragon and serve piping hot.

Chilli Sauce

This is very hot, but marvellous in small amounts or as an addition to other sauces.

> 6 hot red chillies, chopped finely, including seeds
> 4 large onions, chopped very fine
> 3 lb (1½ kilos) peeled tomatoes
> 6 tablespoonsful raw sugar
> 3 tablespoonsful sea salt
> 25 fl oz (710ml) cider vinegar

Boil gently for an hour, stirring frequently. Pour into warm jars. Seal.

Cole Slaw Sauce (for use with white or red raw shredded cabbage)

Shake the finely shredded cabbage with some vinaigrette dressing to which has been added an extra large pinch of mustard.

Alternatively use the recipe for Favourite Dressing, p. 49.

If covered the cole slaw will keep several days in the fridge.

A little shredded raw beetroot is an improvement both to the flavour and texture.

Mint Sauces

Take a large enough bunch of mint, wash clean, take off the leaves, chop fine (we use a cheap gadget of French origin). Add, for four people, one teaspoonful raw sugar, cover with cider vinegar. Leave for at least half-an-hour before using.

Mint jelly is also very tasty. To do that add 1 tablespoonful gelatine crystals to 4 fl oz (100ml) hot cider vinegar. When dissolved, add 4 fl oz (100ml) cold cider vinegar together with raw sugar and mint as above.

Poivrade Sauce (hot, for vegetarian roasts)

> 1 large chopped onion
> 2 grated carrots
> 3 tablespoonsful chopped parsley (or 1½ tbs. dried)
> 2 tablespoonsful corn oil
> ½ bay leaf
> pinch thyme

Cook together for five minutes or so.

Add: 5 fl oz (150ml) red wine

3 tablespoonsful cider vinegar.
Cook until reduced to half.

Add: 12 fl oz (350ml) thick brown gravy. Cook for half-an-hour. Strain into clean saucepan with a pinch of ground cloves and 2 teaspoonsful freshly ground black pepper. Stir well and cook gently for five minutes more.

Sorrel Sauce

A traditional accompaniment to vegetables. This recipe is seventeenth-century.

Crush about 3 oz (75g) of chopped sorrel with the flesh of two peeled eating apples. Beat in a teaspoonful of raw sugar and a tablespoonful of cider vinegar. No need to cook this one!

Sweet and Sour Sauce

(Beloved of the Chinese and good with many fried things and under-cooked vegetables.)

    8 tablespoonsful cider vinegar
    8 tablespoonsful honey
    1 small green pepper (sweet) chopped fine
    1 tablespoonful chopped almonds or cashew nuts

Mix and heat gently before serving. You can also add a clove of crushed garlic. If you prefer a milder sweet and sour sauce, add up to half-a-pint of stock to taste.

Worcestershire Sauce

Most recipes for this famous sauce contain a lot of anchovies, which are not to every taste. Here is a well-tried method, too extravagant for the commercial producer. A cheap sherry, preferably dry, is good enough.

2 teaspoonsful pimento
1 teaspoonful clove
1 teaspoonful black pepper
1 teaspoonful ginger
1 teaspoonful chilli powder
1 oz (25g) curry powder
2 oz (50g) mustard
2 oz (50g) bruised shallots
2 oz (50g) sea salt

   8 oz (225g) raw sugar (dark)
   4 oz (100g) tamarinds
   1 pint (575ml) sherry
   2 pints (1 litre) cider vinegar
   a touch of caramel to colour

Use whole spices where available. Bruise them by roughly pounding. Simmer everything, except the sherry, together for an hour. Top up with more cider vinegar if any has been lost by evaporation. Add the sherry and any colour needed (caramel from heating sugar and water together). Leave for a week. Coarsely strain and bottle.

CHUTNEY, PICKLES AND MUSTARDS

You can substitute cider vinegar for ordinary vinegar in any recipe, but here are some tested and occasionally unusual ways of making these excellent accompaniments.

Apple Chutney (An old Devon recipe)

   40 fl oz (1 litre) cider vinegar
   2 lb (1 kilo) apples (cored and peeled)
   1 lb (450g) raw sugar
   1 lb (450g) raisins (seedless)
   2 teaspoonsful sea salt
   1 lb (450g) onions
   1 oz (25g) mustard powder
   1 teaspoonful cayenne

Chop all ingredients coarsely. Boil until tender, about one hour. Pour into hot jars. Seal.

Apple and Blackberry Chutney (another Devon treat)

   1½ lb (675g) apples (cored and peeled)
   1½ lb (675g) blackberries
   10 fl oz (275ml) cider vinegar
   ½ lb (225g) raw sugar
   1 teaspoonful sea salt
   4 oz (100g) raisins (seedless)
   4 oz (100g) sultanas
   2 cloves crushed garlic or

3 small chopped onions
1 teaspoonful ground ginger

Crush the blackberries in the pan with the vinegar. Simmer for twenty minutes and rub through a coarse sieve (or use a colander). Add the other ingredients. Cook gently until thick, this takes about forty minutes. Pour into hot jars and seal.

Green Tomato Chutney

This recipe was devised by Martlet. None of the garden-grown tomatoes ripened one year so we tried this recipe and found it very good.

4 lb (2 kilos) green tomatoes
1½ lb (675g) onions
1½ lb (675g) apples (after peeling and coring)
1 lb (450g) sultanas
2 lb (1 kilo) raw sugar
2 oz (50g) mustard powder
4 oz (100g) sea salt
1 oz (25g) ground ginger
1 oz (25g) crushed garlic
1 teaspoonful cayenne pepper
juice of 2 lemons
2½ pints (1½ litres) cider vinegar

Slice the tomatoes, apples and onions thinly. Mix well with the other ingredients. Simmer for 2 hours or until well cooked and thick.

Bengal Apple Chutney

This is highly spiced and a first-rate accompaniment to curries and savouries.

3 pints (1¾ litres) cider vinegar
1 lb (450g) raw sugar
2 oz (50g) mustard seed
8 oz (225g) raisins (seedless)
2 oz (50g) garlic
8 oz (225g) onions
7 lb (3 kilos) cooking apples
2 tablespoonsful sea salt
½ oz (15g) chilli powder

1 teaspoonful cumin powder (if available)
2 oz (50g) fresh ginger *or*
4 teaspoonsful powdered ginger

Scrape the ginger, but mind the eyes whilst you do it! Mince it with the onions and garlic. Core, slice and peel the apples. Simmer the apples with the cider vinegar and raw sugar until the apples are quite soft. Add everything else and simmer for another twenty minutes, stirring frequently. Bottle.

Tomato Ketchup

Ketchup is a modern word for thin chutney. In about 1690 it was called *catchup*. In the 1730s the name became *catsup*, which is often still used in America. Only in the last century was ketchup made commonly with tomatoes. Before then, walnuts and mushrooms were the usual basis.

3 lb (1½ kilos) tomatoes
2 oz (50g) sea salt
1 pint (575ml) cider vinegar
2 oz (50g) raw sugar
2 teaspoonsful mustard powder
1 teaspoonful pepper

Peel the tomatoes by plunging them first into boiling water for a second. Chop them coarsely, sprinkle with the sea salt and allow to stand for at least 3 hours. Boil with the other ingredients for half an hour, stirring frequently until thick and smooth. Fill into clean bottles whilst still hot. Keep for a few days before using.

Hot Peach Chutney

This is best made with slightly unripe peaches. If you do not want it hot, replace the chilli and ginger by a teaspoon of mustard powder and ¼ teaspoonful of pepper.

2 lb (1 kilo) peaches
1 lb (450g) raw sugar
1 pint (575ml) cider vinegar
8 oz (225g) sultanas
1 oz (25g) chilli powder
1 teaspoonful ginger powder

Skin the peaches. Halve them and remove the stones. Bring half the cider vinegar to the boil with the raw sugar. Lower the halved peaches into the liquid. Simmer until they are soft. Add all the remaining ingredients. Simmer until thick. Bottle. This is best matured for a few weeks to bring out the flavour. The recipe is worth trying with plums. These do not need peeling.

Pickled Onions

In olden times you used a silver knife for peeling the onions as steel discolours the flesh. Today stainless steel is fine. We like our onions crisp. If you prefer yours softer then cook them for 5-7 minutes in the spiced vinegar before bottling.

After you have peeled the onions, cover them with water to which has been added 3 ounces (75g) sea salt for every pint (575ml). As the onions like to float, put a plate on top to keep them down. Leave the onions at least twenty-four hours — forty-eight hours or longer does no harm — before thoroughly draining them.

Spiced Vinegar is best made at the same time as you brine the onions. You can buy ready mixed pickling spice which is very good, but if your prefer to make your own use, to every quart (litre) of vinegar: ¼ ounce (7½g) allspice, ¼ ounce (7½g) blade mace, ¼ ounce (7½g) cinnamon sticks, 20 peppercorns and, if liked, ¼ oz (7½g) root ginger in the piece, plus four or five whole dried red chillies.

You can either tie the spices in a bag of muslin (in which case add ¼ oz (7½g) cloves) or you can, as we do, bottle the spices with the onions. The first way looks best. We prefer the flavour the second way. In either case, simmer the spices in the vinegar for an hour, with the lid on a stainless steel saucepan, and leave to cool and mature until the onions are ready for bottling. Pack the dry onions carefully into sterile jars (leaving the empty jars for an hour in the oven on gas mark 1 or electric 275°F (140°C) and allow to cool). Pour on the spiced vinegar and store in a cool place.

This method works also with cauliflower, green tomatoes and cucumbers.

Piccalilli

3 lb (1½ kilos) green tomatoes

½ lb (225g) cabbage
1 lb (450g) cauliflower florets
1 large cucumber
4 medium sized onions *plus*
   20 pickling onions if available
2 tablespoonsful sea salt
2 pints (1 litre) cider vinegar
1 lb (450g) raw sugar
3 teaspoonsful turmeric
4 oz (100g) mustard powder
1 teaspoonful black pepper
2 oz (50g) tapioca starch or
   if not available, cornflour

Mix the tapioca or cornflour in a little cider vinegar then simmer the rest of the ingredients for fifteen minutes. Turn off the heat, add the cider vinegar/tapioca or starch mixture and allow to cool. Chop all the vegetables and place the layers in basins with layers of sea salt between. Let this stay overnight. Drain off the liquid completely. Mix the sauce and the vegetables thoroughly. Put into sterile jars, seal carefully. Ready for use in two weeks.

Pickled Crab Apples
This recipe works with any small sour apple, but it is a good way of using crab apples.

5 lb (2¼ kilos) crab apples
1¾ pints (1 litre) cider vinegar
2 lb (1 kilo) raw sugar
pickling spices in a bag (see page 61)

Stir the sugar into the cider vinegar, drop in the spice bag, and bring to the boil in a container that is not aluminium. Simmer gently for twenty minutes, removing any scum that forms on the surface.

Trim the ends of the apples, wash carefully and add to the simmering mixture. Continue cooking until the apples begin to soften. Pack them into jars without any liquid which then has to be reduced until it becomes syrupy. Pour over the apples whilst still hot and then seal securely.

Pickled Red Cabbage

For this wonderful preparation which is a splended accompaniment to many savoury dishes both hot and cold you will need:

    4 lb (2 kilos) red cabbage
    5 oz (350g) sea salt
    10 shredded bay leaves
    2 tablespoonsful black peppercorns
    2 oz (60g) sliced fresh ginger root
    1 oz (25g) allspice
    cider vinegar as necessary

Prepare cabbages by slicing them thinly and chopping them up. Spread them out into flat non-metallic dishes, sprinkle with sea-salt, then lightly cover with a cloth or kitchen paper. Let it stand for twenty-four hours.

Drain the cabbage through a large sieve, cover again and leave for a further day with the occasional shake. Sprinkle the spice mixture all over the cabbage so that it is well mixed but not bruised. Gently put the mixture into jars without pressing down. Leave some room above the top of the cabbage. Cover with cider vinegar which needs to be quite cold.

It is important to be sure that the jars used are very clean indeed and that, after filling, you seal down very firmly so that no air can get in. The pickle is ready to eat within a month and is well worth waiting for.

Pickled Eggs

Cider vinegar has the special property of preventing discolouration of the eggs. All you have to do is to gently boil the eggs for twenty minutes, shell them while still quite hot and drop them straight into cider vinegar in a storage jar.

Pickled Fish

Pickling is a wonderful way of preserving the valuable naturally occurring fatty acids found in all fat fish. These acids help to protect against heart disease. With many fish you can use far more herbs and spices than with the simple recipe for pickled herring on page 76.

Prepare the fish yourself or ask your fishmonger to fillet whatever fish seems the freshest and best when you are buying. Remove the backbone and any dark flesh and cut up the fish into pieces two or three inches long and put them into a large pottery or glass (not metal) jar.

For every 1 lb (450g) fish add two heaped tablespoons of sea salt. Cover with cider vinegar, stir and leave in cool room temperature for four or five days.

Pour away the liquid and put the fish into a large container with copious amounts of fresh water overnight. Remove and give a final rinse and return to the cleaned jar.

Meanwhile prepare a pickling mixture sufficient to cover the fish. For every pint of cider vinegar you will need one teaspoon raw sugar, ½ teaspoon coriander, ½ teaspoon cumin, ¼ teaspoon black pepper, ½ teaspoon dill, ½ teaspoon allspice, 6 bay leaves, 1 small chopped onion, half a lemon including the peel.

Cook together in a stainless steel pan simmering gently for one hour. Allow to cool. Pour over the fish, cover securely and refrigerate for at least one week before eating. This should keep in a cool place for several months.

Rollmops

Soak herring fillets in brine, just as for pickled onions, with 3 ounces (75g) sea salt to each pint (575ml) of water, but with the addition of 2 tablespoonsful of cider vinegar to each pint (575ml). Leave them for four hours in a cool place. Then replace the brine with cider vinegar with 1 ounce (25g) sea salt per pint (575ml), and leave for a further twelve hours. Finally wrap each fillet round some shredded onion and fasten the tail with a cocktail stick. Put in fresh cider vinegar with some herbs or spices, especially paprika and bay leaves, if you like. They will keep for four weeks in the fridge.

Mackerel in Vinegar

Fillet the fish. Dry them by dredging with flour. Fry in corn oil until golden. Leave to cool. Put a layer of the fish into a bowl, sprinkle with sea salt and raw sugar then another layer of fish and so on until all is used. Slice an onion thickly, put this over the top layer, sprinkle with pepper. Cover with cider vinegar. Leave in a cool place for two or three days. Taste the vinegar adding more raw sugar if required. This keeps for weeks in a cool place.

English Mustard

Instead of mixing powdered mustard with water, use cider vinegar. Allow the mixture to stand for about half-an-hour to develop the flavour. Mustard tastes better and keeps longer this way.

German Mustard

Take 2 ounces (50g) mustard powder with 1 ounce (25g) cornflour or tapioca flour. Mix in a large pinch each of ginger powder, ground cloves, ground caraway seeds, a teaspoonful of sea salt and two of raw sugar. Make the lot into a fairly thick mustard by gently cooking it with half a pint (225ml) of cider vinegar. Allow to cool and store in small sealed pots.

DRINKS

There are some old ways of using cider vinegar as an essential ingredient for a refreshing summer drink.

Cowslip Cider Vinegar

Collect a quarter of a pound (110g) of cowslip 'pips', as the flowers are called, pull them from the stalks, cover with a pint (575ml) of cider vinegar and allow to marinade for three days. Strain the liquor through a fine sieve or some muslin into a stainless steel or enamelled saucepan. Add 1 lb (450g) of raw sugar and stir until dissolved. Put the lid on and stand the pan in a larger pan of boiling water. Cook like this for an hour, topping up the water, as necessary. Bottle when cold. It is better if you add a wineglass of brandy to each pint (575ml)! Dilute with soda or ice cold water, as required.

Elderflower Sparkling Wine

You will need 2 heads elderflowers in full bloom, 1 lemon, 2 tablespoonsful cider vinegar, 1 gallon cold water and 1½ lb (675g) raw sugar.

Squeeze the lemon and put with the quartered peel into a non-metal container. Add the other ingredients and leave for twenty-four hours. Strain and pour into clean, screw-top bottles. Keep for a least two weeks before using.

Fruit Cider Vinegars

Many people in olden times thought a drink of a diluted fruit cider vinegar was a good winter health promoter. You may like to try the idea. You can use any soft fruit, raspberries and blackcurrants being especially nice. You can use up the small or squashed fruits very well this way. Use one pint (575ml) of cider vinegar to each pound (450g) of fruit. Mix the cider vinegar and fruit together and stir them from time to time for about five days. Strain the liquid, pressing out as much as possible from the fruit pulp. Add half-a-pound (225g), or more to taste, of light raw sugar to each pint (575ml). Boil for ten minutes and fill into warmed bottles, whilst still hot.

You can use these vinegars as interesting varieties for dressings but they are excellent as a drink, when you may wish to add extra sugar.

SOME OTHER IDEAS
Cheese Softening
In 1577, a certain B. Goodge wrote these words, 'Hard cheese wrapped in cloutes wet in cyder vinegar returns to a softeness.'

Stopping Potatoes Browning
Add a good splash of cider vinegar to the water into which you slice potatoes. When you have finished you can dry them, prior to cooking, with far less chance of their discolouring.

Steaming Vegetables
When you cook vegetables by the healthy method of steaming them (there is less vitamin and mineral loss this way), add 2 teaspoonsful of cider vinegar to the water you use. This helps the vegetables keep their colour without the vitamin C depleting effect that comes from using bicarbonate of soda.

Poached Eggs
We do not care for those moulded eggs which come from bought egg poachers. They seem to lack interest and excitement. Put a saucepan of water on to boil, add two teaspoonsful of cider vinegar and wait until it is simmering gently.

Meanwhile crack one or two eggs into a small container or cup which is less than half the width of the pan.

With a wooden spoon briskly stir the bubbling liquid. When it is going smoothly, gently pour the eggs into the vortex of the little whirlpool that has been created. The whites coagulate nicely and in two minutes you are ready to serve the poached eggs upon wholemeal toast.

Furniture Polish
This is not a joke! Nor have we substituted cider vinegar in a recipe

usually using the ordinary type. The formula, as it stands, is the recommendation of the United States Bureau of Standards.

Cider vinegar	12½ pounds (5¾ kilos)
Petroleum spirits	22½ pounds (10 kilos)
Turpentine	13½ pounds (6 kilos)
Denatured alcohol	2¼ pounds (1 kilo)
Boiled linseed oil	10 pounds (4½ kilos)
Raw linseed oil	12 pounds (5½ kilos)

These quantities produce 10 gallons (45 litres) of polish which should *not* be stored in metal containers because these may be corroded by the cider vinegar. You can use ounces instead of pounds for a smaller quantity of this very economical and good quality polish.

SAVOURY DISHES

Most families love the added aroma and softness cider vinegar gives to so many dishes. Here are a few you may like trying — tastes embrace many ways of eating so keep on tasting until the dish suits you. We are sure there are many folk tales in cookery, one of them is flaming a dish in brandy. This expensive waste can be replaced by a quarter of the brandy, not flamed, added just before you serve. Sometimes a dash of angostura bitters does instead, this is especially good in soups. To start with a real scorcher:

Vindaloo Fish
You require:

    1 lb skinned and filleted fish
    1 teaspoonful mustard powder
    2 teaspoonsful chilli powder
    2 teaspoonsful cumin powder
    6 cloves
    6 cloves of garlic (unless you are frightened)
    2 teaspoonsful turmeric
    1 teaspoonful ginger
    1 stick cinammon
    1 tablespoonful raw sugar
    2 tablespoonsful sea salt

   3 tablespoonsful corn oil
   3 tablespoonsful cider vinegar
   2 large onions

Take all the ingredients except the fish, onion and oil, mix them to a
pulp, crushing the garlic and cloves. Cut up the fish, cover all parts with
the mixture. Leave for at least five hours, a day is better, in a fridge. Fry
the onion in corn oil. Add the fish and spices. Cook in a closed saucepan
until the fish is cooked through. Add an extra sprinkle of cumin just
before serving.

Vindaloo Vegetables
The foregoing recipe can also be used with certain vegetables, either
a mixture or, more successfully, courgettes, aubergines, mushrooms and
sweet peppers and with firm fish such as cod.

Indian Spiced Green Bananas and Potatoes
Green or very unripe bananas are used as a vegetable in many hot coun-
tries. Serve with unpolished rice or wholemeal bread.
   For four people:

   6 green bananas
   6 medium sized potatoes
   1 tablespoonful cider vinegar
   2 large onions
   ½ teaspoonful raw sugar
   4 bay leaves
   2 tablespoonsful corn oil
   2 cloves garlic
   1 teaspoonful powdered ginger
   1 teaspoonful curry powder (or 2 teaspoonsful curry paste)
   sea salt to taste
   ⅛-1 teaspoonful chilli powder

Skin the bananas and boil till soft in a little water. Mash them. Wash
and dice the potatoes, lightly boil in a little water until slightly soft.
Heat the oil and then gently fry the onions until golden, add the spices,
bay leaves and chopped garlic, fry all together for a minute. Then add
the potatoes, bananas, sea salt and raw sugar. Fry gently for five minutes

stirring carefully so as to break up the potato. Add the cider vinegar, stir once more and serve.

Goanese Egg Curry

This recipe comes from the former Portuguese part of India where they would use ghee or clarified butter for the cooking — but it is very good and more healthy with vegetable oil.

  6 hard boiled eggs (cooked and cut in half)
  ½ oz (15g) fresh green ginger
  ½ teaspoonful chilli powder
  1 teaspoonful cumin seeds
  1 cupful cider vinegar
  2 onions (chopped)
  a small piece of cinnamon bark (or a pinch of cinnamon)
  1 teaspoonful garam masala (mixed Indian spices)
  1 tablespoonful molasses or raw sugar
  3 cloves garlic

Pound all the spices except the cinnamon bark into a paste with the ginger, garlic and some cider vinegar. Fry the onion in the oil until it is slippery but not coloured. Add the paste and cinnamon. Continue frying for almost two minutes. Add the molasses (or raw sugar) and cider vinegar. Gently lower in the halved eggs and simmer very slowly until the mixture has become thick.

This looks attractive served hot on a bed of unpolished rice arranged like a sunburst.

Indonesian Pickled Vegetables

These are a fiery accompaniment with an interesting blend of exotic flavours — and easy to prepare.

  4 oz (100g) French or runner beans (chopped)
  2 oz (50g) cauliflower florets
  ½ cucumber (skinned, seeded and cubed)
  6 oz (175g) carrots (in matchsticks)
  2 fresh chillies (without seeds, sliced)
  1 oz (25g) fresh green ginger (sliced)
  3 tablespoonsful cider vinegar
  2 teaspoonsful raw sugar

   1 large onion (thinly sliced)
   2 cloves garlic (crushed)
   ¼ teaspoonful turmeric
   2 tablespoonsful vegetable oil
   1 cupful water

Fry the onion in the oil until golden. Make a paste of the turmeric and garlic and fry it with the onion for a minute while stirring. Add the water, chillies, cider vinegar, ginger and raw sugar. Bring to a gentle boil, add the prepared vegetables and simmer until the vegetables are cooked but still a little scrunchy.

Onion Bhaji
This is good either alone as a tasty appetizer or as an accompaniment to a curry.

   1 lb (450g) onions
   2 tablespoonsful butter or vegetable margarine
   3 oz (75g) 81% self raising flour
   ½ teaspoonful ground cumin
   ¼ teaspoonful ground coriander or garam masala
   ¼-1 teaspoonful (depending how hot you like them) chilli powder
   ¼ teaspoonful sea salt
   1 teaspoonful cider vinegar
   2 tablespoonsful (approx) water

Chop the onions then mix in all the ingredients except the water. Use just enough water to make a thick dough. Compress the mixture into shapes like small eggs.

    Lower them gently, one at a time, into deep hot vegetable oil so that they are covered. After four or five minutes they will be crisp. Take them out gently and let them drain. Serve hot.

Chinese Fried Vegetables
The quick preparations of the Chinese kitchen help preserve the nourishment and bring out the flavours.

   5 oz (150g) leeks
   5 oz (150g) carrots
   5 oz (150g) celery
   5 oz (150g) turnips

5 oz (150g) French or runner beans
1 teaspoonful cider vinegar
¼ teasponful sea salt
1 tablespoonful vegetable oil
1 teaspoonful sesame oil (or vegetable oil if you have no sesame)

Cut the beans into 1 inch (2.5cm) length. Thinly slice the other vegetables into strips. Heat the oil, add the vegetables and stir slowly over a good heat for five minutes. Add the cider vinegar and sea salt and carry on frying for two to three minutes more. Can be served hot or, better still, cold with the sesame oil as a dressing.

Mixed Nuts Curry

This is excellent with unpolished long-grain rice. The best way to prepare the rice is to rinse it well in a sieve under running water. Bring a large saucepan of water, containing a sprinkle of sea salt, to the boil and then add the rinsed rice to the bubbling water. Simmer for 20-25 minutes, then drain through the sieve. The rice will be tender and separate.

For the curry you will need (for four people):

2 medium onions (chopped)
1 tablespoonful curry paste
  (or ½ teaspoonful curry powder)
12 oz (350g) mixed nuts (skinned)
1 tablespoonful cider vinegar
1 teaspoonful yeast extract
½ teaspoonful sea salt
2 tablespoonsful sultanas or raisins
4 fl oz (100ml) corn oil
1 chopped red sweet pepper
  (or 3 chopped tomatoes) — for colour
2 teaspoonsful molasses
12 fl oz (350ml) water
2 tablespoonsful wholemeal flour

Fry the onions in the corn oil until slippery. Add the curry and simmer for two minutes, stirring. Add the nuts and continue cooking and stirring for a further minute. Stir in the raisins and the flour with a little water. Cook for another minute, then add the rest of the ingredients (except for the pepper or tomato) and simmer for five minutes. Add the pepper or tomato and serve at once on a bed of rice.

Including the preparation of the vegetables, this meal can be ready within 35 minutes.

Curry Paste

Curry powder is best when freshly ground and many Indian suppliers have their own blend. At other times a tin of curry powder is a good substitute because it is sealed at the factory.

Having used the powder once it begins to age and the delicate aromatic flavours become less distinct and delicate. If you prepare your own curry paste the flavours are preserved very well.

A good way of making a curry is to gently fry some chopped onions in a heavy pan, or casserole, then add the curry powder or paste and fry the mixture for another couple of minutes whilst stirring. Now add your other ingredients plus enough liquid and simmer until cooked.

Here is the recipe for curry paste.

  8 oz (225g) curry powder
  14 fl oz (400ml) cider vinegar
  3 fl oz (75ml) corn oil
  1 oz (25g) raw sugar
  1 teaspoonful ground cumin seed

Heat the oil in a thick pot. Add the spices and fry very gently for three to five minutes, stirring all the time. Add the raw sugar and cider vinegar, mix thoroughly, bottle and seal. Curry paste keeps well.

Sweet and Sour Mixed Vegetables

A key element of good healthy cooking is to go shopping without too many preconceived notions of what you are going to purchase. The right foods to buy are those which look best and are the most economical on the day. When shopping recently for some cod to make sweet and sour cod we found that, because of the glut in the market, salmon was cheaper! So economy turned to economical luxury.

So many wonderful vegetables are available from around the world that you can ring the changes, always bearing in mind colour and texture when mixing.

This sweet and sour dish can be stir fried in a wok or in a shallow large frying pan:

½ lb (225g) baby carrots
2 different colour capsicums (sweet peppers)
4 oz (100g) mushrooms (preferably small button)
1 bunch spring onions (scallions)
½ lb (250g) beansprouts
2 tablespoonsful runny honey
2 tablespoonsful cider vinegar
3 tablespoonsful corn oil
1 teaspoonful coriander

Prepare the vegetables by scrubbing or scraping the carrots, chopping up the capsicums and trimming the spring onions so that a good part of the green remains. (Never buy spring onions with tired looking green leaves.) Heat the oil in the wok or saucepan, add the carrots and cook over a medium heat, stirring gently for three to four minutes. Add all the other vegetables except the beansprouts and increase the heat and continue stirring for a further three minutes. Add the ground coriander (You can use an old electric coffee grinder to prepare spices directly from the seed which is so much more aromatic), the honey and the cider vinegar. Stir well to coat the vegetables. Add the beansprouts and cook for a further minute. Serve at once.

Rice Salad

You can use mushrooms or prawns instead of the anchovy fillets, if your prefer. Take:

½ lb (225g) brown rice (basmati is best;
    patna almost as good)
2 oz (50g) tin anchovy fillets
4 oz (100g) olives (stoned: black are best)
3 tablespoonsful cider vinegar, sea salt, pepper
1 sliced tomato
1 cupful cooked green peas

Cook the rice in lots of boiling, sea salted water. After twenty minutes fish out a grain and test it for softness with your finger nails. Do this again each minute until the rice has softened moderately. Drain the rice through a sieve, wash with cold running water. Drain completely, put

in a basin until cold. Add the other ingredients having mixed the oil,
cider vinegar, pepper and sea salt. Stir gently until completely mixed.
Decorate with a sliced green pepper or tomato.

Fish Shashlik

Take and cut into large cubes enough firm fish for your needs. Put the
fish to marinade for about half a day in enough cider vinegar to cover,
with lots of raw onion rings and a teaspoon of coriander.

Skewer the cubes. You can, if you wish, alternate the fish with green
peppers, mushrooms and sliced tomatoes. Brush with corn oil and grill
on a hot flame until done. Serve with the onion rings from the
cider vinegar, sprinkle with cumin seed and perhaps a little salt and
paprika.

Almond and Garlic Soup with Grapes

A Spanish recipe, from Malaga where the grapes are sweet. There they
use freshly shelled almonds dried slightly in the oven and then powdered. We use the less beautiful shop-bought ground almonds, but the
soup is an interesting summer starter.

    2 tablespoonsful ground almonds
    6 cloves garlic
    2 tablespoonsful corn oil
    1 pint (575ml) water
    1½ tablespoonsful cider vinegar
    8 ice cubes
    2 teaspoonsful sea salt
    1 lb (450g) skinned, seeded grapes
    ½ cupful wholemeal breadcrumbs

Pound together with garlic, almonds, salt and oil until smooth. Add the
cider vinegar, grapes, water and ice cubes. Leave one hour in a cold place
before serving.

Gazpacho Soup

This most famous Spanish cold soup comes from Andalusia. You can
either pound the solid ingredients together, apart from the cucumber,
then add the oil drop by drop until it becomes thick when you stir in
the cider vinegar and add the cucumber; or you can save trouble by

using a blender to do your initial blend, adding the oil whilst still blending. If it is too thick, add some water. Add the ice. Chill before serving and garnish with chopped parsley or chives. You need:

5 tomatoes
4 cloves garlic
½ cupful cider vinegar
1 chopped onion
sea salt and pepper
½ cucumber, finely chopped
1 cupful wholemeal breadcrumbs
1 sweet red pepper, chopped
8 ice cubes

Cold Potatoes

An excellent accompaniment for savouries of all sorts.

1½ lb (675g) small new potatoes (unpeeled)
1 tablespoonful corn oil
2 tablespoonsful cider vinegar
2 tablespoonsful chopped chives or onion
1 tablespoonsful chopped parsley

Cut the potatoes into pieces and sprinkle with the parsley and chives or onion. Season with sea salt and pepper. Add the mixed vinegar and oil. Coat gently and serve when cold.

Boiled Salmon

This way does just as well for lobster which takes fifteen minutes in the simmering liquor. Salmon takes about twenty minutes, then you let it cool, in the fridge, in the juice. This makes the salmon very moist and it will keep for a day or so if needed.

Slice 2 onions, 2 carrots and a leek, if you have it, into ¼ pint (150ml) of cider vinegar, plus half-a-pint of white wine, or water will do. Add 3 pints (1¾ litres) of water, a large handful of parsley with about a third as much thyme and two bay leaves. Grind in some black pepper. Bring to the boil and simmer gently for an hour. Put in the salmon and simmer until done. It is often easier to lower and raise the fish on a piece of muslin.

Pickled Herring — Swedish Style

You will need:

 2 small or 1 large salt herring
 1 large sliced onion
 3 tablespoonsful raw sugar
 1 cupful cider vinegar
 ¼ cupful water
 3 bay leaves
 ½ teaspoon white pepper

Soak the herrings in cold water overnight. Dry them and then remove the skin and bones. Slice them into equal sized narrow pieces, arrange them in a dish. Mix all the other ingredients together and pour them over the fish. Cover and leave in a refrigerator for at least eight hours for the flavours to blend.

Spanish Grilled Mushrooms

Put the required number of mushrooms, which have been carefully washed, in a dish and then sprinkle them with olive or corn oil and season with sea salt and fresh ground black pepper. Allow the mushrooms to marinade in this mixture for several hours giving an occasional gentle stir.

Take out the mushrooms, grill them under a hot grill (broil in the United States) until they are just cooked. Transfer them to a warm serving dish. Fry two or three chopped cloves of garlic and some parsley in the marinading mixture, some chives can also be added with advantage, stir in one tablespoonful cider vinegar, pour the sauce over the mushrooms and serve at once.

Cacik (Turkish Cucumber Soup)

You need for this very nice cold soup (which might have been invented by a health food cook):

 1 peeled halved and seeded cucumber
 3 × 5 oz (150g) cartons plain yogurt
 2 teaspoonsful cider vinegar
 1 small teaspoonful corn oil
 milk
 2 teaspoonsful chopped mint

Grate the cucumber and blend it with the yogurt (or put them in a liquidizer). Season to taste, add the oil and cider vinegar. Mix well, then thin to the required consistency with cold milk.

Chill well and just before serving put into cold bowls and sprinkle with the chopped mint.

Chapter 6

CIDER VINEGAR IN THE TREATMENT OF ANIMALS

As we have implied, this section is the key to the whole cider vinegar system of treatment. The allergy specialist, Dr Erik Anderson, who had many reports of the effective use of cider vinegar, honey and beeswax among his patients, said that it has become a rule of thumb in tests which include placebos (that is, treatments using an ingredient which the patient believes is the one that will work, whereas an inert alternative is used instead) that up to a third of the placebo group frequently feels an improvement.

What we humans experience when we are ill is often reduced, aggravated or maybe even caused by our mental processes. We have no reason to believe that cows, pigs, sheep and horses fall into this psychologically motivated category. Yet cider vinegar works very regularly in some common animal complaints. It is used regularly by farmers who certainly cannot afford to waste money on an outside chance of improvement.

This gives good reason to believe that the remarkable results observed from the use of cider vinegar in man are not just faith healing but are a real and positive contribution to sound health.

Many theories have been proposed as to why cider vinegar works and it may be that there is not one answer but several. More research is required and is being undertaken in certain areas of study, such as asthma. A most interesting and exciting recent observation what that one of the causative organisms of mastitis in the cow, *Streptococcus mammitis*, when grown in the laboratory, is killed by the application of a small amount of cider vinegar. In response to enquiries, the chemist said that neither ordinary vinegar of the same acidity nor cider itself had this effect. Here then is a suggestion that there is something very special about cider vinegar. In this connection, the suggestion has been made that the natural balance of phenols and tannins in the acetic cider vinegar is not all that different from the basic chemical materials from which scientists produce bacteria-destroying drugs. The thought this raises is the profound idea that through the use of cider vinegar you enable the body to produce within itself valuable substances for its own protection. It will take many years to test the truth of this proposition, but it is a most provoking suggestion. The chemist in question, Mr Loates of Whiteways, gave his view on cider vinegar and the farmer.

CIDER VINEGAR AND THE FARMER

In these days of antibiotics and synthetic drugs for treatment of both human and animal ailments, the use of natural remedies has been neglected.

For many years the curative and beneficial properties of country remedies were well known and well used, and undoubtedly they had effects which could not be ignored. The great increase in the use of Whiteways Cyder Vinegar by stockmen for treating cattle and pigs during the past few years has shown that these natural remedies do work and are well worth trying.

In primitive areas of France and other parts of Europe, the use of cider vinegar remains a traditional treatment for many cattle ailments. Cattle, sheep, deer and other related animals have a specialized digestive process, and it is upon the proper and efficient functioning of this that the health and condition of the animal depends.

McAnally and Phillipson have dealt with this matter extensively and it might well be of interest to state the basic principles involved. The animals nourish themselves upon grass and similar plant life whose chief contribution is in the form of fibrous carbohydrate cellulose. The indigestible nature of such plant material makes it necessary for large quantities of food to be taken in by the animal in order that its body may obtain sufficient digestible material for its needs.

The digestion of cellulose is accomplished, not by the secretions from the glands of the animal, but by bacteria which inhabit the alimentary canal and which break down the complex carbohydrates into readily assimilable products. The enlarged and elaborated portions of the canal of such animals enable the passage of the ingested material to be delayed at optimum conditions of temperature, moisture and acidity for the action of the bacteria to accomplish the digestive process.

The ruminants have developed for this purpose a stomach divided into four areas, and normally the solid food is swallowed as grazed into the rumen where it may be retained for up to several days. It is subjected to a constant churning and mixing caused by muscular contractions after which it is brought back into the mouth and thoroughly chewed before passing again to the rumen where the finer particles pass on through the omasum to the abomasum, where further digestion takes place.

The chief bacterial process achieved in the rumen is the breakdown of cellulose and carbohydrates to simple organic acids and gasses. The chief of these is acetic acid which is absorbed into the blood-stream, thus providing a source of energy directly from the cellulose. Protein and amino acids are synthesized and stored in the bacteria themselves which pass on and undergo further digestion in the intestine. Vitamins can also be synthesized by the bacteria of the rumen and contribute essentially to the well-being of the animal.

It has been suggested that the formation of acetic acid in the rumen promotes cudding, which ensures the proper working of the digestive system, and the addition of small quantities of cider vinegar to the feed provides the necessary acidity to ensure this. Loss of appetite and cessation of cudding indicates that the rumen has ceased or slowed down its action, due perhaps to badly balanced rations or too finely ground foods. The composition of concentrates can encourage the production of substances in the rumen which retard the normal bacterial action and cider vinegar is able to replace the naturally formed acid and so assist the normal digestive process.

Acetonaemia is a condition of accumulation of fat in the liver which results in certain breakdown products of the fat — ketones — being released into the blood-stream. One of these, acetone, creates the sweet smell noticed in the cow's breath and milk that is characteristic of the condition.

Its cause is said to be an insufficiency of the right sort of substances which prevent the liver from oxidizing the fat in the normal way. These substances consist essentially of sugars broken down from the cellulose in the rumen. It appears to be associated with lack of adequate roughage, and high-yielders fed with a below minimum ration of roughage, to enable them to consume a full concentrate ration, are often prone to digestive troubles and acetonaemia.

Some stockmen add sugar or molasses to the feed to control this condition, but the production of natural sugars by feeding a good ration of hay, at least 6 lb per day for high yielders, with an acidified (cider vinegar) concentrate, is likely to be more effective.

The generally recommended dose is 2 fl oz (50ml) of cider vinegar twice a day, poured over the feed. Larger doses are recommended in acute cases, up to 4 fl oz (100ml) twice a day, which can do no harm.

Dr D.C. Jarvis was the first to systematically investigate the effects of cider vinegar on large groups of cattle. He considered that it helped to maintain a correct balance between the acids and alkalis in the animal's body chemistry. He found this to be of crucial importance in building up resistance to many common farm-yard illnesses. At first he thought that the potassium content was the effective factor, so he carried out experiments which showed that the cider vinegar had a good effect not obtained from the use of potassium alone. I shall deal with some of the most successful uses of cider vinegar in animal treatment. Although the animals are dealt with individually, the experience of one is often applicable to another. It is therefore worth looking for any condition not specifically considered in the section devoted to other animals.

FOR CATTLE

Unquestionably the greatest agricultural use for cider vinegar is in the treatment and prevention of common ailments amongst cattle and for improving general condition, milk yield and fertility.

The usual dose for adult animals is about four fluid ounces (100ml) per day which may be given as just over two tablespoonsful, twice a day.

If the animal is suffering from poor appetite, the cider vinegar can be used as a drench with equal quantities of warm water. A drench —

for the non-farmer — is a liquid given directly into the mouth of the animal from a bottle which has usually a rubber or plastic end. This can be given twice a day until the appetite is restored when the mixture can be poured over the concentrated rations.

Younger or smaller animals require proportionately less. Heifers at bulling age need two fluid ounces (50ml) once a day, weaned calves one fluid ounce (25ml) a day and new-born calves two teaspoonsful each day.

LET THE FACTS SPEAK FOR THEMSELVES

Mr John Waring, who has a herd of pedigree Friesians at Kilnwich Percy in Yorkshire, wrote to Whiteways about his experience with cider vinegar and his record-breaking cow *Winton Pel Eva II*. Here is his letter in full:

Three years ago the above cow appeared on television being one of the few cows to produce 100 tons of milk. An elderly lady who had seen the programme wrote to me. Apparently she had been connected with Jersey cattle in New Zealand for some fifty years. She said I would know what would take my cow as indeed we all know that all cows from about 12 years start to get arthritis and it is the one immobility for which they have to be destroyed. In fact they get down and cannot get up. It was purely through an accident that they found a cure for this, or indeed a prevention.

A number of cider barrels had been left to steep for several weeks and the residue was eventually poured through the fence into a field. The Jersey cows ate the grass and some of the soil. After this they prepared something similar and this they found prevented arthritis.

From that day on we started to feed 2½ pints of cider vinegar per week to the above cow. She is now sixteen years old with no sign of arthritis whatsoever. She is in calf with her thirteenth calf and never looked fitter. She has now produced 138 tons of milk. The World Record, held by an American Holstein, is 145.6 tons. My cow is now well within striking distance and, all being well, this time next year she will have done it.

Another point of interest, after being on cider vinegar she never had milk fever again, and at all previous calvings we nearly lost her.

My vet said on the first occasion it was a coincidence but after the next two calvings has never mentioned it again.

We get a lot of visitors to see the cow and numerous people with old valuable cows are going on to it, as indeed a lot of elderly people themselves are taking it. I wonder if you have noticed any significant increase in sales.

I brought this up at the National Cattle Breeders Club at Cambridge last week and this stimulated a lot of interest but, as there were a lot of professors and doctors etc. in the veterinary world present, they tried to play it cool. But I am certain it really captured the interest of the Cattle Breeders and they are going to try it.

I had fifty Canadians here this summer and they said arthritis took most of their old cows at about fourteen years. The mother of my cow is buried in the orchard here. She went down with arthritis at 16½ but apart from that was perfectly healthy and would have lived several years more.

Yours sincerely
John Waring

TREATMENT OF MASTITIS

Both *Streptococcal* and *Staphylococcal mastitis* seem to be improved by cider vinegar although, as pointed out earlier in this section, the successful laboratory tests have been upon the more resistant *Streptococcus mammitis* not upon the antibiotic-sensitive *Staphylococcus agalactiae*.

The trouble with antibiotic treatment, apart from the cost, is the effect upon the milk because of the unacceptable residue of antibiotic formed therein.

Treatment with cider vinegar by means of a daily ration or drench of up to eight fluid ounces (225ml) a day for three days, then half as much, usually produces clear, clot-free milk within seven days. A regular daily dose prevents further attacks. The milk can be sent to the dairy as soon as it is normal. Milk is never tainted nor harmed in any way from the use of cider vinegar.

When the shape or texture of a quarter of the udder is badly affected it may take up to eight weeks to return to normal. However it has recently been reported that an injection of 5ml of cider vinegar directly into the infected quarter will reduce nodules and clear up infections almost immediately. Prevention and early treatment is best.

The treatment usually seems to work even when the infection is resistant to antibiotics. Some case histories illustrate this point.

Farmer W.J.E. of Haverfordwest learnt his skills from a cowman who came from the Cambridge University Farm who had always used cider vinegar for mastitis. He completely cured two of his cows and quite a few of his neighbour's which were still seriously ill even after massive doses of antibiotics from the veterinary surgeon.

Farmer J.C.O. of Axminster wrote that he had used it on his cattle for years, two tablespoonsful twice a day on their nuts. Before doing this they had terrible mastitis and warble fly.

Farmer R.J.I.W. who has a herd of Ayrshires in Cheshire used the Milk Marketing Board cell-count test to find sub-clinical mastitis. He had been using cider vinegar successfully for some time for clinical mastitis but was worried to find from the tests that a high incidence of invisible mastitis affected the untreated part of the herd. He then treated them all with cider vinegar. The first result was that many of the sub-clinical cases became clinical, but then all cleared up. He thought this might be a step in the elimination of the infection.

Farmer K.J.R. of the Isle of Wight after using cider vinegar on his forty-five Ayrshires for two years was able to say that mastitis had become a rare occurrence.

In the magazine *Dairy Farmer* for December 1967, Mike Walsh wrote how he had, like other readers, successfully used cider vinegar for mastitis but found his results to be not always consistent. He says it is useful in restoring a cow's appetite and also not expensive.

He goes on to mention that an eggcupful every morning will soon have any dairy farmer with rheumatism skipping around like a newborn lamb. And if the dairymaid has a slimming problem she will find it very useful although she will have to watch out for the rejuvenated dairy farmer!

A supplier of cider vinegar to Cumberland farmers relates how after a trial lasting just three weeks he thought cider vinegar wonderful stuff because it had completely cleared up a persistent mastitis problem. Furthermore, the cows had a bloom he had never ever experienced in the past.

MILK FEVER

Even when animals have a history of repeated severe attacks of milk fever, a daily four-ounce (100ml) ration of cider vinegar given from six weeks before until three weeks after calving has been completely successful in preventing the condition.

ACETONAEMIA

This condition often arises from an unbalanced diet. The liver normally, with the particular aid of certain carbohydrates, oxidizes fats. In acetonaemia it is unable to do this because of a shortage of these carboydrates. The result is that various breakdown products of fat called *ketones* are released into the blood stream. Acetone is one of these and it causes a peculiar sweet smell of the breath and milk that is a characteristic of this disease, the other name for which is ketosis.

Glycerine and propylene glycol have both been recommended as treatments. Yet cider vinegar seems to provide an even better answer. It can be used as a preventative by giving two fluid ounces (50ml) twice daily from three to six weeks before calving until four to six weeks after. As a treatment drench with eight fluid ounces (225ml) of cider vinegar mixed with an equal quantity of warm water on the first day. On the second and successive days give 4 fl oz (100ml) diluted with an equal quantity of lukewarm water until normal appetite returns, and then add 2 fl oz (50ml) twice daily with the feed. To prevent a recurrence of the attack continue treatment for at least ten days.

Mrs E.M.C. of Calne, writing in *Farming Express*, said that her dairy herd had suffered from acetonaemia for many years. They tried both glycerine and potassium chlorate without satisfactory results even thought they were expensive. She had read an article in the *Daily Express* discussing the properties of cider vinegar almost two years earlier and her family had used it ever since. She has seen her cows eat their cake within an hour of being drenched. She gives ¾-pint (425ml) or ½-pint (275ml) of cider vinegar according to animal size and there is rarely any loss of milk.

The paper's veterinary adviser thought that her results were a result of supplying the cow with the necessary organic acids which are normally present in ruminal fermentation.

IMPROVED MILK YIELDS AND CONDITION

Mrs Marrable of Marle Green, Sussex, who has a herd of twenty milking Friesians and Shorthorns, first tried small quantities of cider vinegar late in 1964. Here are her results for that and the succeeding two years:

	1964/65	1965/66	1966/67
Milk yield (lbs)	10,085	10,509	11,507
Butterfat per cent	3.61	3.59	3.56
Veterinary fees	£45	£15	£15

After the second year she wondered if other factors might have produced these changes, so she waited another year before feeling confirmed in her findings, which were published in *Farmer and Stockbreeder* in December 1967.

Mrs Marrable showed the reporter how keen the cows were on cider vinegar by tipping a small quantity on the grass when they gathered around to lick it up as eagerly as they would eat linseed cake.

This herd's fertility has improved and there have been no calving troubles or retained cleansings. The calves themselves appear extra vigorous and go to a local dealer who is prepared to pay slightly higher prices because of their sturdiness and good coats. All the cattle on the farm have the supple skin and shining coat so valued by stockmen.

Dr Jarvis found even greater increase in milk yields over a similar period, but his herd may have been in a worse condition at the start than Mrs Marrable's.

DRYING OFF IN MILK COWS

Mastitis is common at this time, and as I have indicated, cider vinegar is a valuable preventative. It has been suggested that drenching can be avoided at this time if a very small ration of concentrate, even as little as six cake nuts, is placed by the cider ration in the manger. Once this becomes an established routine the cows often drink the vinegar from their manger without any concentrate in addition. The period of preventative treatment varies with the quality of hay or pasture providing maintenance, and the milking potential, from between one and three weeks. It is usual to give four fluid ounces (100ml) a day for the first week and then half as much for as long as necessary.

FERTILITY

Users universally report improved fertility from heifers and cows when they are on a four fluid-ounce (100ml) daily ration. This is particularly striking in the high first service conception rates in both bulling heifers and cows. Yet other farmers do not find a regular dose so effective as giving one pint of cider vinegar on the concentrate just before serving.

Stock bulls on a regular four fluid-ounce (100ml) daily ration tend to maintain semen of high fertility even during slack periods. The treatment also stimulates bulls who are uninterested.

We have previously referred to the report of Mrs E.M.C. in *Farming Express*. She says that she gives cows half-a-pint (275ml) before service and had all her cows and heifers in calf during the last winter. The vet said he was not certain of the action of cider vinegar on fertility, the possible explanation being the rich mineral properties of the vinegar, particularly the trace elements which may be of value in breeding efficiency.

No one seems to have tried this application on people!

ARTHRITIS AND RHEUMATISM

More and more farmers are reporting success in the treatment of arthritis and rheumatism even when the cattle have been too lame or stiff to rise or to graze effectively. Two ounces a day of cider vinegar has given cows destined for the stewpot several years of active happy life with useful milk yields. It is very important to give the dosage *regularly*.

A DYSENTRY TYPE SCOUR

Mr I.E.V. of Ellesmere wrote to say that he had a seven-year-old Jersey cow who, for no apparent reason, began a dysentry type scour. The vet was called in, he says, and treated it with an armoury of drugs and drenches. As soon as the treatment ceased the cow immediately became worse again. 'I then decided to try my own herbal medicines. I drenched the cow twice a day with four fluid ounces of cider vinegar, a large tablespoonsful of pure honey all in a half-a-pint of warm water. After three days the cow had started to chew her cud which was something she had not done for five days on orthodox veterinary treatment.' At the time of writing he said that the cow was still improving steadily and he is now putting cider vinegar in her drinking water.

PIGS
Farrowing Fever

For prevention in susceptible sows, give them two fluid ounces (50ml) a day for from two to three weeks prior and one to two weeks after farrowing. The piglets are usually more active and the sow does not lose her appetite. If she has farrowing fever then give two ounces (50ml) daily for at least ten days.

Farmer G. Chatham of Kingsbridge found he was constantly having large veterinary bills because of farrowing fever. His losses of pigs and consequent debility were very bad. He used the two fluid ounces (50ml) for two weeks before and one week after treatment and reported a marked improvement in his breeding stock. Since using cider vinegar he had no cases of farrowing fever or similar udder troubles. The young pigs were more lively and less laid on by sows. Since using cider vinegar he was of the opinion that both the quantity and quality of his pigs had greatly improved. He has asked that his experience be shared with other breeders to cut their losses by such a simple but safe treatment.

Scouring

As with calves, bacterial and nutritional scouring is often cured with cider vinegar in the drinking water of pigs.

Farmer K.J.R. of Newport, Isle of Wight had one pig which was scouring so badly it was almost dead. Ten days after the cider vinegar treatment was begun, the pig was back to normal.

Farmer D.F.W. of Chard has twenty-two breeding sows, some three years old. In the past he has had to have the vet two or three times to each at farrowing time. Now sometimes the vet comes once and sometimes not at all. He is having better litters with nine to twelve reared. His vet's bill is down by two-thirds.

Incidentally, just before farrowing, he gives the sow either a pint (575ml) of stout or one-and-a-half pints (750ml) of rough cider and finds this makes them so docile that they lie down and farrow half asleep!

GOATS

In general, the treatments for goats are about half that for cattle.

Mr J.L.R. of Colchester who has a herd of dairy goats, found cider vinegar particularly effective in the treatment of acetonaemia.

POULTRY

Turkeys and chickens have been reported to show an improved rate of growth when a teaspoonful of cider vinegar is added to each quart (litre) of drinking water.

Mr John Woods of Preston, a poultry keeper on a considerable scale, made a controlled trial on birds in battery cages which had poor shell texture following respiratory infection. He added the cider vinegar at 1 per cent, that is two-and-a-half gallons (10½ litres) per ton of feed.

The addition was known to no-one but himself and his mill operative and he frankly said that he had little confidence of any beneficial results. He checked the shell texture at the end of two weeks with no apparent change. Almost as an afterthought, he checked again at the end of a month and found a most marked improvement. He assessed the number of cracked and porous eggs was reduced by 80 per cent in the treated group.

HORSES AND PONIES

The suggested doses are three fluid ounces a day for small ponies, horses up to fifteen hands four fluid ounces (100ml), and over fifteen hands six ounces (175ml) per day. As many horses are rather conservative in their eating habits it is best to give it with their favourite food. Drenching is not recommended for horses and ponies with cider vinegar or with other fluids for that matter, unless it is done by a veterinary surgeon, as the procedure can lead to respiratory complications.

LOST APPETITE

A ration that is high in concentrates frequently causes horses and ponies to become bored, when they lose interest in their food. The use of cider vinegar on the feed often stimulates the appetite as well as improving the general condition.

DUNG EATING

This rather unpleasant habit is clearly discouraged by the rapid removal of the dung. It could be, however, that it has a nutritional origin because a course of cider vinegar, which is rich in minerals, often cures the condition.

COAT CONDITION

Horses and ponies improve the suppleness and bloom of their coat when on a course of cider vinegar in a significant number of instances.

POISONING

Because of the effect that cider vinegar has both in improving the appetite and in restoring the intestinal organisms that are so often altered or destroyed either by accidentally-eaten poisons or veterinary treatment with a similar effect — for example, antibiotics often damage the bacteria essential to good health even though they may be necessary for treatment — there will be gradual but helpful assistance from the use of cider vinegar in such circumstances, when used in addition to the usual procedures.

EQUINE INFLUENZA AND COUGH

We have noted only one communication upon this subject, but very interesting.

Lord C. from Dorset writes that he has been feeding cider vinegar to horses for a number of years and although they have mixed freely with sufferers from cough or equine flu, they have so far been immune. Perhaps this is a result of the cider vinegar treatment.

CIDER VINEGAR WORKS WONDERS FOR RACEHORSES

The famous racehorse *Noble Dancer*, who in 1978 won £200,000 ($400,000) in prize money, was a regular user of cider vinegar for health and fitness. More and more trainers are giving their thoroughbred horses cider vinegar and saying that it keeps them in the peak of condition in a quite remarkable way. Indeed several trainers have told us of their experiences with cider vinegar but forbidden us from mentioning their names or their horses because they want to keep this secret weapon to themselves! However, it can be revealed that *Noble Dancer* takes Martlet cider vinegar whereas the famous racehorse trainer, David Morley from near Bury St Edmonds insists that the cider vinegar for all his horses must be made from Aspall organically grown cider vinegar.

Today, many leading horse owners including famous regiments and members of the Royal family as well as leading trainers have become regular users for their livestock and praise the importance and value of cider vinegar.

SHEEP
Twin Lamb Disease

This is a toxaemia of pregnancy which usually occurs in ewes in the fourth and fifth months of pregnancy, often when they are carrying two or three lambs. When contracted, it is frequently fatal so prevention is important. The incidence has been said to reduce when two fluid ounces a day of cider vinegar are sprinkled over the concentrate. Treatment is certainly worth trying by using a drench with quarter-of-a-pint (150ml) of cider vinegar and an equal amount of warm water and then the two ounces (50ml) a day for one or two weeks.

USEFUL ADDRESSES

Appleford Limited
325 Oldfield Lane North
Greenford
Middlesex UB6 0AZ

Aspall Cyder House Products
The Cyder House
Aspall Hall
Stowmarket
Suffolk IP14 6PD

Martlet Health Food Products
Horam Manor
Horam
Heathfield
E. Sussex TN21 0JA

Whiteways of Whimple Limited
The Orchards
Whimple
Exeter EX5 2QJ

INDEX